ECONOMIC GROWTH
AND ECONOMIC POLICY
IN A MULTINATIONAL SETTING

ECONOMIC GROWTH
AND ECONOMIC POLICY
IN A MULTINATIONAL SETTING

The Habsburg Monarchy, 1841-1865

Thomas F. Huertas

ARNO PRESS

A New York Times Company

New York / 1977

Editorial Supervision: ANDREA HICKS

———•———

First publication 1977 by Arno Press, Inc.

Copyright © 1977 by Thomas F. Huertas

DISSERTATIONS IN EUROPEAN ECONOMIC HISTORY
ISBN for complete set: 0-405-10773-0
See last pages of this volume for titles.

Manufactured in the United States of America

———•———

Library of Congress Cataloging in Publication Data

Huertas, Thomas F
   Economic policy and economic growth in a multinational setting.

   (Dissertations in European economic history)
   Originally presented as the author's thesis,
University of Chicago, 1977.
   Bibliography: p.
   1. Austria--Economic policy. 2. Austria--
Economic conditions. 3. Austria--History--1789-
1900. I. Title. II. Series.
HC265.H83   1977   330.9'436'04   77-77174
ISBN 0-405-10787-0

THE UNIVERSITY OF CHICAGO

ECONOMIC GROWTH AND ECONOMIC POLICY IN A

MULTINATIONAL SETTING: THE HABSBURG

MONARCHY, 1841-1865

A DISSERTATION SUBMITTED TO

THE FACULTY OF THE DIVISION OF THE SOCIAL SCIENCES

IN CANDIDACY FOR THE DEGREE OF

DOCTOR OF PHILOSOPHY

DEPARTMENT OF ECONOMICS

BY

THOMAS FRANCIS HUERTAS

CHICAGO, ILLINOIS

MARCH 1977

ACKNOWLEDGMENTS

I wish to gratefully acknowledge the assistance and encouragement given me during each stage of my work by the members of my thesis committee, Robert W. Fogel, Harry G. Johnson, Arcadius Kahan and Donald McCloskey. In addition I would also like to thank Emil Karafiol of the Department of History for his extensive comments on an early draft of the dissertation.

I would also like to thank Professor Alfred Hoffmann and Professor Michael Mitterauer of the University of Vienna who kindly made available to me the resources of the Institut für Wirtschafts- und Sozialgeschichte during my stay in Vienna. While in Vienna I also benefited from lengthy discussions with Professor Eduard März, Dr. Roman Sandgruber and Professor Herman Freudenberger.

Financial assistance from the Ford Foundation and the New York State Board of Regents made my studies at the University of Chicago possible. This I gratefully acknowledge.

Lastly, I would like to thank Altheia Chaballa for her careful typing of the dissertation.

TABLE OF CONTENTS

LIST OF TABLES

GLOSSARY

CM   Conventionsmünze, the currency standard in use in the Habsburg
        Monarchy until 1858.

fl.   Gulden.

OW   österreichische Währung, the currency standard in the Habsburg
        Monarchy after 1858 (1 fl. CM = 1.05 fl. OW).

WC   Wiener Centner = 100 Wiener Pfund = 56 kg.

ZZ   Zollzentner = 100 Zollpfund = 50 kg.

BNS   Bollettino di notizie statistiche.

MGS   Mittheilungen aus dem Gebiete der Statistik.

SAV   Statistisch-administrative Vorträge.

WZ   Wiener Zeitung.

ZVRZV   Zeitschrift des Vereins für die Rübenzuckerindustrie im
        Zollverein.

INTRODUCTION

The Habsburg Monarchy[1] was an anomaly in nineteenth century Europe,
a supranational construct in a world of nation states, which ultimately
collapsed under the pressures of its diverse national movements. Could such
a state harbor or even promote the forces of economic growth? Many nineteenth century observers believed the answer to be no; as evidence they
pointed to the increasing economic gap between the Monarchy and the German
national state (Treue, 1975).

-----

[1]The Habsburg Monarchy consisted of three parts, Cisleithania, the
lands of the Hungarian Crown and Lombardy-Venetia (cf. map). The first
covers the territory officially known after 1867 as "Die im Reichsrath
vertretenen Königreiche und Länder." Specifically, this included the provinces
of Upper and Lower Austria, Salzburg, Carinthia, Tirol (including Vorarlberg),
Styria, Bohemia, Moravia, Silesia, Galicia (including after 1846 Krakau),
Bukowina, Carniola, the Littoral (Görz, Gradisca, Istria and Trieste) and
Dalmatia. Dalmatia formed a separate customs area until 1879. The lands of
the Hungarian Crown included Hungary proper as well as Croatia-Slavonia and
Transylvania. The Military Borderland was technically ruled directly from
the War Ministry in Vienna, but I have included it under Hungary. Lombardy-
Venetia, the Monarchy's two Italian provinces, also formed a separate adminis-
trative unit. In 1859 the Piedmontese and French wrested Lombardy away from
the Monarchy; in 1866 the Piedmontese added Venetia to the newly created
Italian state.
　　　　Prior to 1848 these three units--Cisleithania, Hungary and Lombardy-
Venetia--were also the administrative subdivisions of the Monarchy. Under
the dictated constitution (oktroyierte Verfassung) of 1849 Cisleithania and
Hungary formed a unitary, absolutist state. Beginning in 1860 the Monarchy
underwent a series of constitutional experiments which culminated in the
Compromise (Ausgleich) of 1867. This created two states, Hungary and
Cisleithania, under the personal dynastic union of the Habsburg Emperor-
King Francis Joseph.
　　　　It is important to note that the provincial boundaries did not
correspond at all to the contours of the various nationality groups within
the Empire. Cf. Kann (1950).

Until recently, this also remained the opinion of most economic historians who dealt with the Empire (Matis, 1972; Tremel, 1969; März, 1968; Brusatti, 1973; März, 1957). They ascribed the Monarchy's relative economic backwardness to her inability to overcome natural and historical barriers to progress. The growth which the Empire did achieve they attributed to the partial removal of these obstacles. In the last ten years several historians have undertaken to estimate the actual record of Austrian economic growth (Gross, 1966, 1968a, 1968b; Good, 1974; Rudolph, 1973). Their research shows that the Monarchy, or at least its western half, experienced substantial industrialization and growth in the seventy years preceding its demise in World War I, although at a slow but steady pace rather than via a spectacular take-off or big spurt.

In these investigations the period before 1867 has been relatively neglected. A closer examination seems required in view of the great importance which the more traditional economic historians attach to the neo-absolutist reforms of the 1850's as a preparation for a possible take-off. The period 1841-73 also coincides with the German take-off; comparison with the German experience may yield an insight into the causes of Austrian backwardness.

This study, therefore, reviews the record of Austrian economic growth in the period 1841-1865. It finds that the Austrian economy was growing rapidly in the period 1841-1857, which suggests that the Austrian economy was already engaged in the process of industrialization and growth, and that the 1840's and 1850's were more than a preparatory epoch. The study then assesses the impact of the economic reforms of the neo-absolutist era--were they the cornerstone of later progress? The answer turns out to be no, at least for the major trade reforms, i.e., the formation of a unified customs area (1850),

the tariff reductions (1852, 1854) and the commercial treaty with the
German Zollverein (1853). The study concludes with a brief comparison
of the Austrian and the German economies and suggests that differences
in monetary and fiscal policy, rather than the failure of Austria to join
the Zollverein, may offer an explanation of Austria's relatively sluggish
economic growth.

To a great extent the economic policies of the Habsburg government
were in reaction to nationalist movements inside and outside the Monarchy
and dictated by the dynasty's attempt to maintain and broaden its influence
within Europe.[1] The attempt to secure domestic unity in order to obtain
international power is not a problem restricted to nineteenth century
Central Europe. Indeed, the parallels between the Austrian case and the
situation confronting many developing countries and Europe itself today,
lend it more than an antiquarian interest. Hopefully, the study will permit
a greater insight into the costs and benefits of economic integration.

---

[1]For a summary of Habsburg foreign policy in a European context
see Taylor (1973); Böhme (1966). For a Habsburg perspective and for
domestic policy see Kann (1950); Redlich (1920); Zöllner (1970).

CHAPTER I

AUSTRIAN ECONOMIC GROWTH, 1841-1865

The first attempt to quantify nineteenth century Austrian economic growth and hence to gauge accurately the Empire's relative backwardness dates back only ten years. In his pathbreaking doctoral dissertation Nachum Gross (1966) applied the methods of modern national income accounting to the data contained in the industrial surveys of 1841, 1866, 1880, 1885 and 1911/13. The resulting estimates of industrial value added and national income (for 1841 and 1911/13) afforded a broad outline of Austria's economic development which supplemented the existing histories of the Monarchy's institutions and policies. Gross documented a substantial increase in real industrial value added per capita in the period 1841-1911/13.

According to his calculations industrialization took a slow start; in the period 1841-1865 per capita value added grew at 2.25 percent per annum. This meshes well with the traditional assessment of the 1840's and the 1850's as a foundation for the future economic advance. After 1865, the pace of industrialization quickens to over four percent per annum, a reflection, Gross believes, of the boom in the Grunderjahre (1867-1873), which outweighed the depression following the stock market crash of 1873. Growth of industrial value added slackened somewhat after 1880 to 3.4 percent per annum. Overall, per capita industrial product grew at a rate of 3.05 percent in the years 1841-1911. Rudolph (1973) and Good (1974) have suggested that this rate of industrial expansion, although slow, was fairly steady in the period 1873-1911/13.

4

TABLE 1

ANNUAL RATES OF GROWTH OF REAL VALUE ADDED PER CAPITA
IN THE INDUSTRIAL PRODUCTION OF CISLEITHANIA, 1841-1911

	(1) Estimates of Nachum Gross		(2) Revision
1841-1865	2.25%	1841-1856/8	3.6%
1865-1885	4.09%		
1880-1911	3.42%		
1841-1865	3.08%		
1865-1911	3.46%		
1841-1911	3.05%		

SOURCE: Column 1: Gross (1966, p. 64). Column 2: See text.

The same hypothesis cannot be advanced for the period immediately
before 1873. Gross suggests that the Gründerjahre (1867-73) represented
a sharp break with the past, in which Austria's feudal heritage and natural
handicaps had inhibited economic growth. However, the 1866 industrial
survey upon which Gross based this interpretation was statistically the least
reliable of his data sources, as Gross himself admits.

In fact, the 1866 series of lectures by Friedrich Schmitt upon which
Gross based his estimate of 1865 industrial value added refer to the results
of an industrial survey undertaken ten years earlier in preparation for the
1857 world statistical conference in Vienna. Schmitt had already published
the results of this survey in the 1860 edition of his Statistik des österreichischen Kaiserstaates and the figures in his lectures six years later were
substantially unchanged (Table 15).

Therefore, I have replaced Gross's 1865 estimate with one for
1856/58. This implies that Cisleithania actually achieved Gross's 1865
level of industrial output nearly a decade earlier than he estimated.
As a result, one must revise his low estimate of industrial growth in the
period 1841-1865 and question the epithet sluggish applied to the Austrian
economy of that period. Actually, industrial output was expanding at over
3.5 percent per year, a fairly rapid rate of growth. This indicates that
historians may have overestimated the obstacles to economic growth posed
by Austria's feudal heritage and by her natural handicaps. This in turn
poses the question of the impact of the neo-absolutist regime's institutional
reforms, which were intended to remove these obstacles to economic growth.

Table 16 presents the revised estimate of industrial value added
for Cisleithania, a total of 440 million fl. OW at current prices, approximately 12 percent above Gross's estimate of 392 million fl. The difference
arises primarily from the replacement of Gross's value added coefficients with
those estimated from Schmitt's industrial survey. I also applied these
value added ratios to Gross's estimate of industrial value added in 1841
so that I might calculate a growth rate for the period 1841-1856/8. These
revisions increased the estimate of industrial value added in 1841 by
14 percent (Table 17). In order to calculate real per capita industrial
value added it was necessary to divide the estimates by the population and by
an approximate price index.

The results (Tables 1 and 18) present a strikingly different portrait
of early Austrian industrialization from that of Gross. Real per capita
industrial output in 1856/8 actually exceeds the value estimated by Gross for
1865. This in effect transposes Gross's scenario; rather than a sluggish
preparatory epoch (1841-1865) yielding to a dynamic expansion (1865-1885),

the estimates presented here indicate that an early period of vibrant
growth (1841-1856/8) occurred. The data tenuously suggest that growth
then faltered for the next thirty years (1856/8-1885), when the advance
was somewhat tepid. However in the last three decades of the Monarchy's
existence a moderate pick up in the rate of growth took place.

However, the limited nature of this revision is to be emphasized.
This study leaves open the importance of the Gründerzeit for Austria's
economic development. It also leaves untouched Gross's pattern of long term
economic growth—one of slow but steady industrialization.

Moreover, this revision does not imply that Gross's estimate of
industrial value added for 1866 is incorrect. In fact, some of the production indices for individual industries suggest that the Austrian economy
did stagnate between 1858 and 1865. Chapter IV develops the hypothesis
that the Habsburg Monarchy's military policy, compounded by its contractionary
monetary policy, may have arrested the process of Austrian industrialization.

The 3.6 percent annual rate of growth of real per capita industrial
production in Cisleithania from 1841 to 1856 compares favorably with the
2.8 percent rate which Germany achieved from 1850/54 to 1855/64. Thus,
Austrian industry was growing at approximately the same rate as did the
German during the early stages of its take-off.[1]

This assessment is substantiated by a comparison of the national
income of the two areas. It is possible to combine the estimate of industrial
value added with similar estimates of value added in agriculture, mining and
smelting, commerce, transportation and services to arrive at a figure for
national income. Commodity output amounted to 2.7 billion fl. OW in 1856/58

---

[1]Calculated from index of German industrial production in Mitchell
(1973, p. 768). Rate of population growth from Mitchell (1973, p. 747).

8

TABLE 2

DEVELOPMENT OF THE AUSTRIAN COTTON INDUSTRY, 1841-1861

	Total Monarchy				Monarchy without Italy				
	Yarn Pdn. (Mil. kg.)	Net Yarn Imports (Mil. kg.)	Total Yarn available for weaving (Mil. kg.)	Gross Value of industry production (Mil. Fl. oW)	Factories	Spindles ('000)	Yarn Pdn. (Mil. kg.)	Spindles/ Factory	Output/ Worker (kg.)
1841	12.0	2.65	14.65	21.8	145	900	10.0	6206	565.3
1843							12.9		
1845							15.3		
1846	23.6			63					
1847	20.5				177	1233	16.7	6966	687.3
1849							18.3		
1850	22.5						18.8		
1851	22.5	2.8	25.3		172	1340	19.3	7791	749.9
1854	27.7	2.9	30.6	84	161	1352	23.1	8398	889.0
1857	29.6	8.2	37.8	100	168	1503	25.2	8946	937.7
1859	28.9	4.4	33.3		162	1469	27.8	9068	1066.4
1860				120					

SOURCE: Tafeln, "Gewerbliche Industrie, Baumwollspinnereien," 1841-1859; Denkschrift (1848, pp. 9-10); Arenstein (1862, p. 64); Schmitt (1860, pp. 218-221).

and gross domestic product to 3.7 billion fl. OW or about 110 fl. OW per capita.

Nearly 50 percent of GDP originated in the agricultural sector, about 15 percent in the industrial and about 35 percent in transportation and services. Compared with Germany, the Habsburg Empire had a lower share of GDP in industry and in services and transportation. Total per capita GDP was about 30 percent less than the corresponding figure for Germany.[1]

There exists substantial evidence from individual industries that Austrian industrialization did proceed at a rapid pace in the 1840's and early 1850's, as the aggregate estimates indicate. The most complete evidence comes from cotton and iron manufacture, the two trademarks of the industrial revolution. Examination of their performance also gives some details concerning the path of industrialization.

Cotton yarn production rose to two and one-half times its 1841 level by 1857, an average rate of growth of 5.8 percent. The total output of the cotton industry rose at an even quicker pace--at 6.9 percent per annum, nearly tripling within the period. Nearly two-thirds of the increase in yarn production came in the brief five year span 1841-46 when output leapt from 12.0 million kg. to 23.6 million kg.--a growth rate of 14.5 percent per annum. In the next five years yarn output stagnated but beginning in 1851 the industry expanded once again, although at a more moderate pace (4.7 percent per annum) than during the boom years of the early 1840's.

---

[1]Mitchell (1973, p. 803). Average net social product for Germany in 1856/58 is 8685 million mks. with depreciation of 7 percent this yields GDP of 9320 million marks or 4900 million fl. OW at then current exchange rates; 1857 population estimated at 35.5 million from data in Mitchell (1973, p. 747). This yields a per capital income of 138 fl. OW, approximately 30 percent above the level of the Habsburg Monarchy.

Overall, however, the industry expanded nearly 50 percent in the six years 1851-57, as yarn imports nearly tripled. Thus, the focus of expansion in the cotton industry shifted to weaving.

Although the Monarchy's cotton industry was less advanced than those of England and France it did surpass Germany's spinning branch as late as 1846. The Monarchy had both higher number of spindles per factory and a higher total number of spindles. By 1860 the latter advantage had disappeared under the impact of the large new southern German factories. Still, the average Austrian factory had over 25 percent more spindles than its counter-part in the German Zollverein.[1]

The iron industry also exhibited vibrant growth in the period 1841-1856/8.[2] Just as in the cotton industry, growth came in two spurts; from 1841 to 1847 production in Cisleithania expanded 41 percent (5.8 percent per annum). After a two year hiatus due to the revolution, the iron industry resumed its upward march; production increased 57 percent in the period 1850-1858 (also 5.8 percent per annum). Thereafter, however, output plummeted, touching a low point in 1865 at 190,000 metric tons, the same output it had attained in 1854. Production in the Monarchy as a whole (without Italy) grew at an even more rapid pace: from 1841 to 1847 at 6.3

---

[1] For the cotton industry see the general statistical surveys listed in note 1, page 12 and Grunzel (1898); Pacher von Theinburg (1891); Kubenik (1863); Adelmann (1966); Bormann (1852).

[2] In addition to the general statistical surveys in note 1, page 12 the following relies upon Beck (5 Vols., 1884-1903); Kupelwieser (1886); Friese (1870); Oechelhauser (1852). Concerning the questions of the tariff and Austro-Zollverein customs union as they affected the iron industry see: Ausserung der Represäntanten der karntnerischen Eisenindustrie uber die vom hohen Handelsministerium angestellte Frage über den Anschluss an den deutschen Zollverein (1848); Rosthorn (1865).

percent per annum; and from 1850 to 1858 at 7.0 percent per annum. In the
early 1860's production fell 13 percent—the sharp decline in Cisleithanian
production was nearly compensated for by the rapid expansion of Hungarian
production.

The entire iron industry expanded at an even faster rate than did
the production of pig iron, if one can use the total consumption of pig
iron as a measure. This rose 47 percent in 1841-46 (6.7 percent per annum)
and 137 percent in 1851-58 (11.4 percent per annum). Again, a comparison
with Germany shows that the Habsburg Monarchy equalled the Zollverein in
total pig iron production as late as 1845-49, but that it failed to keep
pace with the spectacular German advance in the boom of the 1850's. In
the early 1860's German production continued to expand while the Monarchy's
iron producers faced a severe slump. This, of course, widened the gap between
the two areas.

TABLE 3

PIG IRON PRODUCTION OF AUSTRIA-HUNGARY AND GERMANY, 1840-1869
(Averages in thousand metric tons)

	Austria-Hungary	Germany
1840-44	142	160
1845-49	180[a]	184
1850-54	219	245
1855-59	299	422
1860-64	331	613
1865-69	336	1012

SOURCE: Table 20 and Mitchell (1973).
Note: [a]1845-47.

Rapid growth in other industries furnishes additional support
for the thesis that Austria experienced rapid industrialization in the
period 1841-1856/8. The manufacture of linen, wool and silk textiles
expanded vigorously during the period.[1] Non-ferrous metals showed moderate
growth in the 1850's.[2] Beer output rose steadily from 1841 to 1865; alcohol
production increased at a 4.7 percent annual rate from 1852 to 1859.[3] The
beet sugar industry mushroomed to five and one-half times its 1850 size
by 1858.[4]

The statistics on coal consumption and the use of steam engines
buttress further the thesis that Austria underwent rapid industrialization
in the 1840's and 1850's. Through their rapid increase one may gauge the

---

[1] This paragraph relies upon several general statistical surveys of
the Austrian economy. These include Schmitt 1st ed. (1854), 2nd ed. (1860),
3rd ed. (1867), 4th ed. prepared by Schimmer (1872); especially Schmitt
3rd ed, pp. 217-48; Arenstein (1862); Kotelmann (1852); Hubner (1850);
von Reden (1846); Hain (2 Vols. 1853). In addition, a note to each of the
tables gives the sources of the figures presented.
Concerning the development of the linen industry see Leiter
(1916); Winkler (1866); von Viebahn (1846). Also see Tables 22 and 23.
For the development of the woolen industry see, in addition to
the general statistical surveys Heym (1864); Migerka (1866); von Viebahn
(1846); Mudge and Hayes (1868). Also see Table 24.

For the development of the silk industry see Tables 25 and 26 in
addition to the general statistical surveys, the reports of the Chambers of
Commerce for Milan, Bergamo, Cremona and Como for the 1850's as well as
Silbermann (2 Vols., 1897); Mulheder (1952); Knoth (1947); Tambor (1876);
Harpke (1876); Frattini (1856).

[2] See the general statistical surveys and Äusserung der Repräsentanten
der kärntnerischen Bleiproduktion über die vom hohen Handelsministerium
aufgestellte Frage, bezüglich auf den Anschluss an den deutschen Zollverein
(1848). Also see Table 27.

[3] For beer brewing see Dessary (pp. 191-228, 1861); Purs (p. 42, ff).
Also see Table 28. For alcohol distilling see Dessary (pp. 55-102, 1860).
Also see Table 29.

[4] In addition to the general statistical surveys see Baxa (1937, 1950);
Baxa and Bruhns (1967); Hubner (pp. 27-30, 1850); Rad (1862, 1864, 1868);
Kutschera (1904); Renhardt (1975). Also see Table 30.

pace at which Austrian industry adopted advanced western technology. In
1863 Cisleithanian industry employed seventeen times the steam horsepower
it had in 1841 (Table 4). Undoubtedly, most of this advance represents
the conversion of older production methods to steam power, but some gain in
total output probably also resulted. Similarly, coal consumption in
Cisleithania rose 10.4 percent per annum from 1851 to 1873, again evidence
of a shift to more modern methods of production and probably an indicator
of an increase in total industrial output.[1]

The trade structure of the Habsburg Monarchy corroborates the
hypothesis that Austria in 1850 was both already relatively advanced
industrially and that it was rapidly making further progress. This runs
counter to the more traditional assessment that the backward techniques
which the Monarchy's industry employed prevented the Monarchy from competing
on the world market. Consequently, in these accounts the trade reforms of
the early 1850's had a major impact on Austrian economic growth, since they
exposed the fragile Austrian industry to the rigors of foreign competition.
In order to combat the influx of imports manufacturers accelerated their
adoption of technical innovations, which in turn quickened the economy's
advance (Matis, p. 34 ff, 1972; März, p. 19, 1968; Tremel, pp. 326-7, 1969;
Lang, pp. 183-4, 1906).

A reexamination of the Austrian trade statistics will lay the ground-
work for a reappraisal of the effects of the trade reforms, as well as add
some broad brush strokes to the portrait of the Monarchy's economy in the
period 1841-1865.

---

[1]Gross (1971) uses this phenomenon as a proxy for industrial production.
At least for the period before 1860, this must be inexact due to the substitution of coal for wood in many industrial and domestic (home heating) uses.
The path of coal consumption follows a logistic curve, typical of those
describing the adoption of a new innovation.

TABLE 4

STEAM ENGINES AND HORSEPOWER IN CISLEITHANIA, 1841-1875

	Total excluding transportation		Total	
	Engines	Horsepower (thousand)	Engines	Horsepower (thousand)
1841	224	2.8	312	7.1
1852	671	9.1	1182	50.0
1863	2882	47.0	4416	335.6
1875	9160	157.3	12390	1275.1

SOURCE: M. Pigerle, "Die Dampfmaschinen und Dampfkessel in Österreich mit besonderer Berücksichtigung von Nieder-Österreich 1841-1881," Statistische Monatsschrift VIII (1882), p. 541.

In general, the Monarchy's foreign trade may be described as the export of finished manufactures and the import of intermediate goods alongside an exchange of products within the primary group.

Throughout the period the Monarchy was a net exporter of finished manufactures. This situation persisted even after the removal of the import prohibitions in 1852; indeed exports of finished manufacturers rose from 1854 to 1862 by 60 percent in real terms (Table 5). And the improvement was general; practically every branch of industry showed an increase in real exports (Table 31). Imports of finished manufactures remained small relative to exports of the same products, although imports did increase rapidly after trade liberalizations of 1852 and 1854. Machinery, books and fine silk goods were the most prominent exceptions to the rule. In 1863 manufactures and processed foodstuffs comprised nearly half of the Empire's total exports but only one-fifth of its imports (Tables 32 and 33). Just as consistently the Monarchy imported intermediate goods throughout the period. Cotton and woolen

TABLE 5

REAL EXPORTS OF MANUFACTURES, TOTAL MONARCHY, 1851–1862

1852 = 100

1851	68.8
1852	100.0
1853	109.9
1854	105.9
1855	126.9
1856	135.1
1857	138.1
1858	118.7
1859	124.9
1860	157.8
1861	173.2
1862	168.6

SOURCE: Table 31.

yarn, pig iron, tanned leather and raw sugar led the import lists. Until
1859 the Monarchy exported significant quantities of silk yarn; in the early
1850's this accounted for 35 percent of total exports. Afterwards, once
Lombardy had been lost, the Monarchy began to import yarn. After 1860 the
Monarchy began to export linen yarn. In 1863 intermediate goods accounted
for 16 percent of imports but only eight percent of exports.

The delineation of primary commodities as imports or exports is not
so clear-cut. About two-fifths of the Monarchy's trade in 1863 involved the
exchange of products within this group. However, the Monarchy did generally
import tropical products such as coffee, spices and sugar, as well as industrial
raw materials such as hides, cotton and sulphur. Exports consisted chiefly
of wool and wood and, after 1856, of grain (wheat, rye, barley; corn remained
an import). Trade in livestock was mixed; imports of pigs were balanced
by exports of cattle.

A closer inspection of Austria's trade performance in finished
manufactured goods belies the label of backwardness applied to its economy,

for it exported a wide variety of such commodities to the Balkans and
the near East, as well as some over the Zollverein border to Germany, the
more advanced industrial West and America. Many export products rested
upon natural resource advantages, such as Bohemian glass and sickles of
Styrian steel. Most manufactures, however, had no particularly Austrian
trait. Austrian textiles, clothing, leather goods and paper competed with
those of the Zollverein and the industrialized West for markets in Balkans,
Italy and the Levant. The existence of a net export trade in manufactures
indicates that Austrian prices for these goods approached the world level.
(Export subsidies did not exist.)

Direct price comparisons between Austrian and foreign manufactures
are unavailable. However, informal comparisons for Trieste, a free trade
entrepôt, suggest that Austrian manufactures successfully competed with a
wide range of English, French, Belgian, German and Swiss products (Der
Freihafen Triest und die österreichische Industrie, pp. 26-30, 1850).
Prussian consular reports furnish additional evidence of this. For example,
the counsul at Livorno reported that Tuscany imported a broad spectrum of
textiles, imitation jewelry (Galanteriewaren) and iron manufactures from
Austria (Handelsarchiv, part 2b, p. 41, 1851). According to the Prussian
representative at Alexandria, Austria shipped woolen and silk cloth, glass
and iron manufactures there (Handelsarchiv, part 1, pp. 427-33, 1851). In
each of these markets Austrian manufactures were able to compete with those
of technically more advanced countries. Austrian finished goods also found
markets in the English "trading preserves" of Syria, Sicily and the Danube
principalities.[1] Thus, the absence of imports of manufactured goods into

-----

[1] Handelsarchiv (1851). Reports of counsuls from these areas are
contained in part 1.

Austria may be traced to the competitiveness of Austrian industry rather
than to the prohibitive system. This price competitiveness also diminishes
the likelihood that the smuggling of manufactures took place on a large
scale.

The low smuggling premiums supply an additional indication that
Austrian prices were comparable to those of their industrial rivals. In
the early 1850's Austrian industrialists estimated the premium at five percent.
In order to compete with these smuggled products, Austrian manufactures
must have sold at approximately the same price, i.e , at most five percent
over the c.i.f. price of foreign goods at the Monarchy's border (Winter, 1850;
Henking, 1850).

CHAPTER II

THE ECONOMIC IMPACT OF THE TRADE REFORMS

The structure of the Monarchy's trade outlined above raises some
question concerning the effects of the government's trade reforms in the
early 1850's. These completely revamped the Empire's foreign trade
regulations. First, the government removed the internal customs barrier
between the Austrian and Hungarian halves of the Monarchy (1850), thus
creating a unified customs area. It then autonomously lowered the tariff
barriers separating the Monarchy from the rest of the world (1852, 1854)
and it tried to merge the Austrian economy with that of the Zollverein in
a Central European customs union. This goal it failed to achieve fully;
it did, however, conclude a commercial treaty with the Zollverein (February
1853).

Historians have labelled these trade reforms as one of the prime
determinants of the political and economic development of the Habsburg
Monarchy. Magyar-nationalist historians have claimed that the removal of
the Zwischenzollinie subjected Hungary to the monopoly of Austrian industry,
thus retarding Hungarian development (Hanak, 1967). Stölzl (1971)
traces the growth of Czech nationalism into a mass movement to the social
disruptions which followed the removal of the prohibitive tariff and to the
consequent influx of foreign goods. Most significantly, historians have
implied that the Monarchy's failure to gain admission to the Zollverein
condemned her to economic sluggishness as well as political impotence (Treue,
1975; Böhme, 1966).

The Removal of the Zwischenzollinie

Until 1850 a customs barrier (Zwischenzollinie) separated the lands of the Hungarian crown from the rest of the Monarchy. Under the provisions of the dictated constitution of 1849 the neoabsolutist government abolished the tariff on intra-Empire trade in an attempt to foster the unity of the Empire.

This step did not silence the debate concerning the benefits of economic integration which had raged between the Hungarian nationalists and the Viennese court during the Vormärz era.[1] Rather, the incorporation of the customs union as the economic cornerstone of the Ausgleich (Compromise of 1867) insured that the debate would remain one of the foremost political issues of the Monarchy until its collapse in 1918.

Economic historians have attempted to assess the importance of this internal customs union for the Monarchy's growth and development. Generally they have stressed its favorable impact upon the Empire's economic progress (Sieghart, 1915; Katus, 1970; Hanak, 1967, 1970; Berend and Ranki, 1970; Hertz, 1947), although a significant minority has emphasized the union's adverse consequences for Hungarian industrialization (Berend and Ranki, 1974; Novotny, 1962; Eddie, 1972).[2]

However, there are two factors which argue against granting the removal of the Zwischenzollinie a major role in the story of Austro-Hungarian economic growth. First, the tariffs on intra-Empire trade were minimal and can hardly be said to have significantly obstructed the economic integration of the Monarchy before 1850. Secondly, most of the goods which Hungary

---

[1]For a summary of this debate see Andics (1973); Barany (1968); Kautz (1876); Sieghart (1915); Beer (1891).

[2]Eddie (1972) argues that the customs union hurt Hungary since it depressed Hungary's terms of trade.

(Cisleithania) exported to Cisleithania (Hungary) were also exported by
the Monarchy as a whole to third countries. This indicates that each
partner's exports were competitive on the world market. Consequently, the
Monarchy also conducted its internal trade at prices close to the world
market level. In combination, these two factors assured that neither
partner incurred a substantial disadvantage from granting preferential
treatment to imports from the other. Nor did either partner gain significantly by having privileged access to the market of the other. For the
Monarchy as a whole the elimination of the Zwischenzollinie brought a
negligible economic gain, since its existence had not greatly hindered an
optimal allocation of its productive resources.

A closer examination of the structure of intra-Empire trade and
of the tariffs exacted at the Zwischenzollinie before 1850 permits an
estimate of the maximum benefit which the Monarchy derived from freeing
its internal commerce. As shown in Table 34, the western half of the
Empire exported manufactured goods to Hungary in exchange for agricultural
products and industrial raw materials.

Manufactures constituted fully three-fourths of Hungary's imports
from the rest of the Monarchy; cotton textiles (31 percent) and other
fabrics (22 percent) accounted for two-thirds of this group. These were
the very products which the Monarchy was selling in the Balkans and Near
East in competition with English, French and German manufactures (see page
16 above).

Consequently, the removal of the Zwischenzollinie allowed Hungary
to import these manufactures at world market prices. Hungarian consumers
benefited from lower prices; the Hungarian economy could also allocate its

resources more efficiently. But these gains were marginal: the low level

of the Zwischenzollinie tariffs insured that Hungary had already enjoyed most of

the benefits before 1850; elimination of the Hungarian import tariff

added less than six-tenths of one percent to Hungarian national income.

Hungary derived somewhat larger benefits from its free access to

the markets of the rest of the Monarchy. However, even these gains were

relatively small: the improvement of Hungarian terms of trade consequent

upon the removal of the internal customs barrier was at most seven percent;

the improvement in Hungarian consumption possibilities at most 1.2 percent

of its national income. The total of the two effects, less than two percent

of Hungarian national income, hardly gave the economy a decisive thrust

onto the path of economic growth.[1]

---

[1]One may quantify Hungary's gain in terms of a two-sector model.
According to an analysis by Jones (1969), the change in real income due
to a tariff change may be expressed as

$$(1) \qquad dy_H = -M_H dB + (T_H - 1) B dM_H$$

where y_H is Hungarian real income, B, its terms of trade (defined as P_m/P_a,
the relative price of manufactures in terms of agricultural goods), M_H, its
imports and T_H, one plus the ad valorem tariff rate on its imports. Changes
in real income arise from two sources. The first term captures the effects
of an increase in the terms of trade; the second evaluates the increased
consumption of importables, whose consumption value $(T_H B)$ exceeds their
alternative opportunity cost (B). It may be shown that

$$(2) \qquad dM_H = -M_H (\varepsilon_H \hat{B} + \bar{\varepsilon}_H \hat{T}_H)$$

where ^ signifies the percentage change in the variable and

$$\varepsilon_H = \frac{\bar{n}_H + \dfrac{M_H}{T_H} + \dfrac{e_H}{T_H}}{1 - m_H \dfrac{(T_H - 1)}{T_H}} = \frac{\bar{\varepsilon}_H + m_H/T_H}{1 - m_H \dfrac{(T_H - 1)}{T_H}}$$

ε_H represents the elasticity of the Hungarian offer curve; $\bar{\varepsilon}_H$, the percentage

For the western half of the Monarchy the merger with Hungary into a single customs area brought a slight loss. In the early 1850's it

---

increase in Hungarian imports at constant terms of trade due to a one percent change in its own tariff. $\bar{n}_H$ is Hungary's compensated elasticity of demand for importables, m_H, its marginal propensity to consume importables and e_H, the elasticity of substitution in production between manufactures and agricultural goods along the transformation curve.

An improvement in Hungary's terms of trade is represented by a fall in $\hat{B}$; the elimination of the Hungarian tariff, by a fall in $\hat{T}_H$. Therefore, both terms in the brackets of equation (2) are negative and Hungarian imports increase as a result of the customs union. We note that $\bar{\epsilon}_H < \epsilon_H$, so that

(3) $$dM_H > - M_H \epsilon_H (\hat{B} + \hat{T}_H).$$

Substitution of this expression into equation (1) yields:

(4) $$dy_H < - BM_H \hat{B} - (T_H - 1) BM_H \epsilon_H (\hat{B} + \hat{T}_H).$$

$(T_H - 1)BM_H$ represents the value of Hungarian tariff revenues; BM_H, the value of intra-Empire trade. $\hat{B}$, the change in the Hungarian terms of trade, is identical with the reduction in the Austrian tariff, expressed as a percentage of the Hungarian price.

(5) $$\hat{B} = \hat{T}_{A'H} + \hat{T}_{AH}$$

where T_{ij} is one plus the tariff rate (t_{ij}) imposed by the ith country on trade with jth. A' denotes an export tax. Thus $t_{A'H}$ is the Austrian export tax on its shipments to Hungary.

Table 18 lists the ad valorem tariff rates for the chief commodities in intra-Empire trade. With the exception of wine and brandy, the maximum rates were:

$$t_{A'H} \leq 1\% \qquad t_{H'A} \leq 1\%$$
$$t_{AH} \leq 6\% \qquad t_{HA} \leq 8\%$$

Substitution of these values into equation (5) yields an estimate for the maximum improvement in Hungary's terms of trade of seven percent and for the maximum decline in Hungary's tariff of nine percent.

The value of Hungarian imports in the pre-March period reached a maximum of 63 million fl. CM. Eddie estimated the short-run elasticity of Hungary's offer curve to have been 0.25 for the period 1883-1913 (1971, p. 307). In view of the similar structure of intra-Empire trade then

relied on third countries to supplement the grain supplies it received

from Hungary. Before 1850 Hungarian exporters paid a lower duty on

---

and in the 1840's, one may adopt this value as a first approximation to that
of ϵ_H. Substitution into equation (4) yields an estimate of Hungary's
maximum gain from the customs union of 4.5 million fl. CM.

Hanak estimated Hungarian national income in 1850 at 391 million
fl. CM., Table 6. Hungary's gain from the removal of the Zwischenzollinie
did not, therefore, exceed 1.2 percent of her national income. Nearly all
(98 percent) of this arose from the improvement in Hungary's terms of trade.

The estimates of the tariff rates given above rely upon 1850 prices.
Since the tariffs on intra-Empire trade were specific levies, the actual
ad valorem rates varied inversely with the price of the traded commodities.
A survey of Hungarian grain prices for the 1840's reveals that the Austrian
import duties fluctuated between three and 12 percent of the Hungarian price.
Even if one employs this larger figure for the improvement in Hungary's terms
of trade, the gain to Hungary from the customs union still does not exceed
two percent of its national income in 1850.

The decline in the ad valorem rates of duty after 1844 was not,
however, due to reductions in tariff rates but to a decline in transportation
costs and to a rise in the relative price of grain as a result of poor
harvests. A possible increase in the general price level may also have
lessened the burden of the specific duties.

TABLE 6

NET NATIONAL INCOME IN THE HABSBURG EMPIRE IN 1850
(in million fl. CM.)

	Cisleithania	Hungary	Total
Agriculture	509	319	826
Industry and Mining	248	45	293
Trade and Transport	136	26	162
Total Net Product	893	390	1283

SOURCE: Hanak (p.268, 1967).

Since Hanak understates the value of national income for 1850, even
the low figures for the static gain from the removal of the Zwischenzollinie
are not a least upper bound. Hanak applies an arbitrarily small 30 percent
as a value added coefficient in agriculture and he relies upon the incomplete
industrial survey of Hain to arrive at his estimate. Another difference with
the 1856/8 estimate presented above is the lower value relative to commodity
output assigned to trade and transportation. Also Hanak estimates net
national income, Chapter I, GNP.

shipments to the western half of the Monarchy than did producers of third
countries. Therefore Hungarians received a higher price for their grain
than did producers in areas outside the Monarchy. The removal of the
Zwischenzollinie increased this differential; this represents the improvement in Hungary's terms of trade mentioned above. The western half of the
Monarchy lost since after 1850 it paid to Hungarian producers this differential; previously this had accrued to the western half of the Monarchy as
tariff revenue. This drop in tariff revenue affords a first approximation
for Hungary's gain and the western half's loss. For the former it amounted
to 0.5 percent of 1850 national income, for the latter 0.1 percent.

For the Monarchy as a whole the loss of its western half counter-
balanced Hungary's gain from the improvement in its terms of trade; the net
gain for the Monarchy as a whole arose from Hungary's elimination of her own
tariff--at most, a miniscule 0.2 percent of the Monarchy's income in 1850.

Yet, it would be false to denigrate completely the economic significance
of the Zwischenzollinie and of its absence after 1850. Although its removal
had a minimal impact on total Hungarian income, the distribution of income
within Hungary may have been altered in favor of the noble owners of large
estates.[1] They formed a bulwark of Habsburg support in Hungary and controlled
the local political scene there both before and after 1848. Thus the removal
of the Zwischenzollinie, which boosted the prices they received for their
grain, may be seen as the central government's reward for their loyalty in

_____

[1]At least in the short run a rise in the relative price of a product
(agricultural commodity) will lead to a rise in price of factor services (land)
which are specific to that industry. In the long run the price of these
factor services will depend upon the capital-labor ratios and input coefficients
in the various sectors of the economy, as well as the elasticity of substitution
in consumption among final products and the elasticity of substitution in
production among the inputs (capital, labor, agricultural raw materials). Cf.
Mussa (1974); Batra (1973); Jones (1971).

the Vormärz period and its attempt to guarantee their faithfulness in the neo-absolutist era.

The suppression of the 1848/49 revolution and the unification of Hungary with the western half of the Monarchy into a single customs area temporarily ended the debate concerning Hungary's economic development which had raged in the 1840's between Magyar nationalists and the Viennese court. Kossuth and his associates in the Schutzverein had demanded the transformation of the Zwischenzollinie into a tariff barrier which would protect Hungarian industry from all outside competition, especially that of the western half of the Monarchy.[1] They predicted this would unleash an industrial boom which would thrust Hungary into the realm of modern states and promote its national identity. Following List, they conceived of an independent tariff as a vital instrument and a proof of national sovereignty.

The association of national prestige with industrial development persisted after the Ausgleich of 1867 so that the customs union between Cisleithania and Hungary still rankled many Magyar nationalists.[2] However, their complaints that the internal customs union hindered Hungarian industrialization were unjustified. The Hungarian government could, and did, resort to direct subsidies to increase industrial output, actually a more efficient means to reach this objective (Offergeld, 1914; Johnson, 1969).

In summary, one must separate the economic and the political significance of the removal of the Zwischenzollinie. The former was negligible;

---

[1]Although demands for a tariff which would protect Hungarian industry had been raised as early as 1833 in the anonymous Umrisse einer möglichen Reform in Ungarn, protectionism found a wide following only after Kossuth began to trumpet its virtues. Cf. Kautz (1876); Andics (1973); Sieghart (1915); Pulsky (1847).

[2]Wolf (1973) summarizes this movement. Cf. also Sieghart (1915).

the latter substantial. Their overlap, the redistribution of income toward Hungarian nobles hypothesized above, remains an important topic for future research.

The Tariff Revisions of 1852 and 1854

As mentioned above, the removal of the Zwischenzollinie is said to have spurred the Monarchy's economic growth through the elimination of internal trade barriers. Similarly, economic historians have emphasized the 1852 and 1854 reductions in the Monarchy's external trade barriers as a significant impetus to its economic advance. The reforms abolished the prohibitive system and permitted the competition of foreign goods within the Monarchy. According to these accounts the influx of imported manufactures forced Austrian entrepreneurs to adopt more advanced techniques of production. This, in turn, boosted productivity and total output.[1]

In fact, the extent of the tariff reform has been greatly exaggerated. For the bulk of Austrian imports duties were actually increased. With respect to manufactures, the reforms at first glance reversed the century old policy of prohibition and substituted a protective tariff in its stead.[2] However, in most cases the government set the rate so high that the resulting duty turned out to be prohibitive.[3]

---

[1] Cf. sources listed in note 1, page 25 and März (1957, 1959).

[2] On the development of the Austrian tariff system see Beer (1891); Grunzel (1912).

[3] In fact, the government itself contended, "Above all one must decisively oppose the assumption . . . that (the 1852 tariff) entails who knows what great and sudden changes in the system which will exercise a convulsive influence on our industrial conditions. This assumption is false through and through." (Austria, kk. Handelsministerium 1851, p. XXVI, my translation). Its determination of the pig iron duty as the amount which would equalize the foreign and the prevailing domestic price (ibid., p. 42) illustrates the objective

In any case, the export performance of Austrian manufactures indicates that tariff reductions on manufactured goods remained without significant effect on the total economy. Prior to 1852 they had successfully confronted foreign competition in third countries such as the Balkans and the Levant. Such competition assured not only that Austrian manufactures themselves sold at world market prices, but also that the impulse for technical improvements reached the Habsburg Monarchy despite the existence of the prohibitive system.

The tariff reform occurred in two stages. The first, in 1852, substituted a protective tariff for the prohibition on the import of finished manufactures which had formed the cornerstone of the Monarchy's tariff policy since the late eighteenth century. However, it went no further than this change of principle; the rates in the new tariff were calculated in order to exclude foreign manufactures from the Empire's market, i.e., they were set at a prohibitive level. The new tariff also left the rates of duty on agricultural products and tropical produce largely unaffected; it merely converted the old rate based on the Viennese system of weights into one based on the Zollverein system and rounded off the resulting figure to an even number. On industrial raw materials such as raw cotton the reform did lower the tariff, but duties on these products were already so low that further reductions had a negligible impact. On intermediate goods such as cotton yarn and pig iron the tariff did offer significant reductions. Others, however, such as linen and woolen yarn experienced duty increases.

Barely two years after the first reform, the conclusion of a commercial treaty with the German Zollverein forced the Habsburg Empire to revise its

---

of the tariff reform: to allow imports in principle, but to price them out of the domestic market. For confirmation see Hübner (1850, pp. 6-7).

external tariff once again. In order to avoid the administrative costs
involved in certificates of origin the Viennese government adjusted its
tariff to the Zollverein level. In order to safeguard its tariff revenues
the Zollverein insisted that the Austrian duties be levied in silver.
Previously, they had been payable in paper currency. This new tariff
regulation raised tariff rates by 22 percent, the premium for silver at
the beginning of 1854.

This was only partially offset by reductions in the level of the
specific tariff. For example, the duty on fine leather was reduced from
15 fl. CM/ZZ to 12 fl. CM/ZZ. The former was payable in paper, the latter
in silver, so that the average duty in 1854 in paper currency after the
silver surcharge was 15.88 fl. CM/ZZ, an increase of approximately six
percent.

However, for most agricultural and tropical goods no countervailing
reduction in the base rate took place, so that the silver clause led to
a 22 percent increase in the rates of duty. Most manufactures also experienced duty increases as did textile yarns, leather and non-ferrous metals.
Only to industrial raw materials, such as raw cotton, hides and sulphur,
did the 1854 tariff reform extend significant new tariff cuts.

In summary, the tariff reforms had little impact on the Austrian
economy. The reduction of duty on industrial raw materials, coupled with
the retention of the same rates for intermediate goods, strengthened the
protection accorded to the modern industrial sector, but also hindered
the development of Austria's export trade in manufactures, since these
were burdened with negative effective protection. The liberalization of
tariffs on imports of manufactures had a negligible effect, since the
Monarchy exported most categories and therefore competed at the world price.

The increase in imports of manufactures was due to intra-industry
specialization and only minimally increased Austria's welfare. Even if
one assumes that the entire increase in imports of manufactures was due
to the tariff change and that the reform halved the Austrian price of these
goods, the maximum welfare gain from the tariff reform was only 0.25 percent
of GNP. Substitution of legal import channels for smuggling routes may
have accounted for the bulk of the increase in the import of manufactures.
If this were the case, the Monarchy had already derived most of the gain
from trade liberalization through the smugglers.

The February Treaty and the Proposed Customs
Union between the Zollverein and the
Habsburg Monarchy

Both the removal of the Zwischenzollinie and the tariff reforms were
intended as stepping stones to the formation of a Central European economic
union of the Habsburg Monarchy with the German Zollverein. Soon after the
suppression of the Hungarian revolt Minister President Schwarzenberg had
refocused Habsburg foreign policy on the fundamental problem of German
hegemony and proposed the inclusion of the entire Habsburg Monarchy in the
German Bund and in the German Zollverein. Prussia correctly saw these
proposals as a threat to its influence in Germany. It not only successfully
avoided the Habsburg embrace but it also used the Zollverein to bind the
samller German states more closely to itself. The exclusion of the Habsburg
Empire from the Zollverein presaged the unification of Germany along Prussian
lines. Austria's commercial setback formed one of the decisive stages in
the rise of Prussia and the slippage of the Habsburg Monarchy from great
power status.

Although the political importance of Austria's exclusion from the
Zollverein has been exhaustively analyzed, its economic impact on the
Habsburg Empire has been relatively neglected, aside from some inferences
that the Monarchy's inability to join the Zollverein condemned it to the
economic backwater. According to this interpretation free trade with the
Zollverein would have brought increased competition for Austrian manufacturers
and opened up new markets for the Monarchy's agricultural products. Thus,
on the one hand, the customs union would have spurred technological progress
in those Austrian manufacturing firms which survived German competition; yet,
on the other hand, it possibly would have made the Habsburg Empire an agricultural appanage of Germany.[1]

In fact, there are solid indications that a customs union between the
Zollverein and the Habsburg Monarchy would have had a negligible impact on
the two areas. And, most of the available gains were actually realized
through the commercial treaty of February 1853 between the two areas.

These conclusions have two foundations. First, the foreign trade
structures of the two areas were practically identical, so that little incentive
for mutual trade existed. Second, the February Treaty slashed duties to a
minimum, so that free trade between the two areas was nearly achieved. The
additional step to a full customs union was economically miniscule, although
politically enormous.

As did the Habsburg Monarchy, the Zollverein in the 1850's exported
finished manufactures and some primary commodities in exchange for inter-

---

[1]Mamroth (1887). These were the fears of Austrian producers of
intermediate products such as cotton yarn and pig iron who dominated the
industrial associations. Of course, they had reason to fear Zollverein
competition, although the producers of final manufactures by and large did
not. Cf. Die Zoll-und Handelseinigung zwischen Deutschland und Österreich
(1850, p. 48); Denkschrift des böhmischen Gewerbevereins über den Anschluss
Österreichs an den teutschen Zollverein (1848, pp. 41-2).

mediate goods, industrial raw materials and tropical products. Textiles
(Table 37) accounted for fully two-thirds of the exports of manufactures;
iron manufactures and glass came next in importance. The Zollverein also
exported significant quantities of grain. Although East Prussia was
beginning to lose its role as England's granary, the Zollverein continued
to ship large quantities of wheat and rye there. In all, agricultural
products constituted approximately 15 percent of total exports.

TABLE 7

TRADE OVER THE AUSTRIAN BORDER AS A SHARE OF TOTAL
ZOLLVEREIN TRADE, 1845-1864
(in percent)

	ZV Imports	ZV Exports
1845	13.5	23.9
1851	13.4	18.1
1854	12.2	16.0
1860	15.7	20.9
1864	19.4	15.3

SOURCE: Borries (p. 47, 1970); von Reden (p. 668, 1854).

Industrial raw materials, such as raw cotton, hides and sulphur
accounted for about 45 percent of the Zollverein's imports. Intermediate
goods, such as textile yarns and pig iron, comprised another 16 percent.
Tropical products (coffee, spices and sugar) had a similar share. Manufactures, in contrast, played a relatively minor role in total imports (12 percent
of the total). Livestock (cattle, pigs) contributed the major share of
agricultural imports.

In its broad outlines Zollverein trade was similar to that of the
Habsburg Empire. Both areas exported manufactures and grain in exchange
for industrial raw materials and intermediate goods. This general similarity
extended to the level of individual commodities with only very few exceptions.

As a result, very little of the Zollverein's trade was with Austria.
Contemporary statisticians estimated that about one-sixth of the Zollverein's
trade took place over the Austrian border (Table 7). Since this included
the Zollverein's trade with the Balkans which passed through Austria in
transit, actual trade with the Habsburg Monarchy was somewhat smaller. The
Budapest Chamber of Commerce estimated that the Monarchy supplied approximately
seven percent of the Zollverein's imports (Bericht der Handels-und Gewerbekammer
Budapest, 1854-1856, p. 89). This corresponds closely to Hübner's (1850)
estimate that the Zollverein conducted about eight percent of its foreign
trade with the Monarchy. According to Zollverein statistics, in 1858 the
Monarchy provided only 9.2 percent of the Zollverein's total imports and
received only 10.3 percent of the Zollverein's total exports (Tables 38 and 39).

The importance of trade with the Zollverein for the Habsburg Empire
is more difficult to assess, since the Monarchy conducted a large portion of
its trade with third countries via the Zollverein. However, the trade which
occurred under the preferences of the February Treaty was separately recorded.
These covered most commodities, so that one may estimate total Zollverein-
Monarchy trade. According to the Monarchy's statistics (Table 22), Austrian
exports to the Zollverein accounted for nearly a third of total Austrian
exports in 1863. The Monarchy received slightly more than a quarter of its
total imports from the Zollverein.

The trade between the two areas involved principally an exchange of
the Monarchy's primary commodities for a wide assortment of Zollverein products.

The Monarchy's principal exports were wool, wood, livestock and grain,
alongside a smattering of intermediate goods (linen, yarn, steel)
and manufactures (linen textiles, glass, books and iron manufactures).
From the Zollverein the Monarchy imported chiefly manufactures (40 percent
of total) and intermediate goods (22 percent), although agricultural commodities
also contributed heavily (38 percent) to total trade. Books constituted
nearly one-fourth of the total imports of Zollverein manufactures, with iron
manufactures, silk and wool textiles, and machinery the other leading items.
Cotton yarn accounted for over 40 percent of the Zollverein's exports of
intermediate goods to the Monarchy.

Although trade with the Zollverein was important to the Monarchy, it
derived little benefit from the privileged access to the Zollverein market
which the February Treaty granted. Not only did the Zollverein itself
export on net most of the commodities which it imported from Austria, but
she also levied only nominal tariff duties on imports of these commodities
from other sources. Hence, the Austrian terms of trade improved little, if
at all, as a result of the February Treaty preferences, since the Zollverein
price equalled or only barely exceeded the world market price. For example,
the Zollverein exempted Austria from its wheat tariff but it levied an
ad valorem duty of only three percent on wheat imports from other countries.
Other primary products had similarly low rates of duty. Wool, Austria's most
important export, was admitted free into the Zollverein regardless of source.

Austria's gain from the February Treaty preferences may be estimated
as the tariff revenues which the Zollverein could have collected, had it
taxed imports from Austria at the nonpreferential rate. These amounted to
0.4 percent of the value of Zollverein trade in 1860-61 or approximately 1.5
million Thaler (3.1 million fl. OW at the then current rates of exchange) or

less than 0.1 percent of the Monarchy's national income in 1856/58.
(Table 42 shows the extent of Zollverein preferences which Austria enjoyed).

Even these minimal gains were offset by the preferences which the
Monarchy accorded to Zollverein products. Despite the preferences the
Zollverein did not exclude other foreign producers from the Empire's market,
so that the tariff preferences failed to induce a decline in the price of
the imported commodities. Consequently, Germany exporters reaped the
differences between the Habsburg duty on Zollverein products and the general
Austrian tariff. Habsburg tariff revenues were lower by an equivalent amount.

However, to the extent that imports from the Zollverein differed
from Austrian products in quality, the February Treaty concessions would
have lowered the Austrian price of such goods. Kotelmann's (1852, pp. 285-6)
description of Austrian manufactures as cheap but of low quality suggests
that the February Treaty may have led to a decline in the relative price of
high quality Zollverein goods such as textiles and iron manufactures. The
consequent increase in Austrian demand would have promoted imports from the
Zollverein and freed additional resources for the export of low quality
manufactures. This increase in intra-industry trade would have benifited
both areas marginally (Grubel and Lloyd 1975, pp. 121-142).

Further extension of the February Treaty into a full-fledged customs
union would have generated little additional benefits for the Habsburg Monarchy
since the commercial treaty had already slashed tariffs on trade between the
two areas to the bone (Tables 36 and 42). Under its terms Austria already
enjoyed free access to the Zollverein market for its most important exports
such as grains, wool, wood, bed feathers, flax, linen yarn, copper, raw linen
fabrics and chemical products. These items accounted for over 70 percent of
the value of exports from the Habsburg Monarchy to the Zollverein in 1863.

The tariffs on the remaining 30 percent of Austrian exports to the Zollverein were not exorbitantly high; rates for livestock, hops, woolen yarn, silk, cotton yarn, fine leather, common glass, flour and fruit all lay below ten percent ad valorem.

The customs union would, however, have further lowered the relative price of high quality products. This would have led to greater specialization within industries and promoted intra-industry trade. Nonetheless, the scope for improvement was small: outside the cotton textile industry the February Treaty had already reduced the tariffs on Zollverein products to very low levels.[1]

In summary, the conclusion of a full scale customs union with the Zollverein would have brought the Habsburg Monarchy little economic advantage. The February Treaty had practically exhausted the production and consumption gains which completely free trade between the two areas would have brought. However, the customs union might have substantially improved the political position of the Habsburg Monarchy. It seems that this prospective political gain motivated Habsburg commercial policy throughout the early 1850's and that the economic benefits of this policy have been exaggerated--both by the publicists of the period and by later economic historians.

---

[1]Kubenik (1863) indirectly acknowledges how little scope for improvement remained, even in the cotton textile industry, in his plea for an increase in the duty on high quality cotton products.

CHAPTER III

THE MONETARY AND FISCAL POLICY OF A
FADING GREAT POWER

Although the Habsburg Empire began to industrialize at a rapid rate
in the period 1841-1856/8, it could not keep pace with Germany. The fault
lay not in its trade regulations; in this area the government practically
exhuasted the small benefits to be had. An alternative hypothesis is that
the government's military struggles to contain the forces of nationalism
and to maintain the Habsburg dynasty's great power status led to monetary
and fiscal policies which impeded economic growth.[1]

This military posture involved the Habsburg Monarchy in five major
conflicts during the eighteen year period 1848-1866. In 1848 nationalist
and liberal revolutions engulfed the Monarchy; only with Russian assistance
could the government finally suppress the last of the revolts in Hungary.
Less than five years later, the Monarchy became involved in the Crimean War.
In order to shortcircuit Russian encroachment upon its sphere of influence
in the Balkans, the Monarchy occupied the Danubian principalities (1854-56).
In 1859 Piedmont won France for the Italian nationalist cause and the two
allies defeated Austria in a short war. The Monarchy was forced to cede
Lombardy to the emerging Italian national state. In 1864 the Monarchy joined

---

[1] Gross (1973) stresses the diversion of resources into war and claims
that trade barriers significantly obstructed technical progress and industrialization. Marz (1957) partly attributes the late nineteenth century boom
to the government's repayment of its bond debt, i.e., the reverse of the
process described below.

Prussia in a successful invasion of Schleswig-Holstein. Two years later the victors fought at Königsberg where Prussia ended the Habsburg claim to German hegemony. Italy also joined the war and wrested the province of Venetia away from the Monarchy.

This succession of conflicts required the Monarchy to limp from one campaign to the next against a fresh enemy. Not only militarily, but also economically, the Monarchy had little time to recover from each war.

Table 8 outlines the rise in government expenditure and revenue during the 1850's. Total government spending rose from 343.4 million fl. CM

TABLE 8

GOVERNMENT FINANCES OF THE HABSBURG MONARCHY, 1850-1860
(In millions of fl. CM)

	Expenditure	Revenue	Deficit[a]
1850	343.4	196.2	147.2
1851	369.5	218.5	151.0
1852	395.7	232.2	163.5
1853	348.3	237.1	111.2
1854	438.1	245.5	192.6
1855	612.7	286.4	326.3
1856	423.8	292.1	131.7
1857	427.7	324.0	103.7
1858	358.5	298.1	60.4
1859	595.5	381.9	213.6
1860	447.3	381.9	65.4

SOURCE: Hübner (pp. 101-102 1861).

NOTE: [a]The deficit is not equal to the public sector borrowing requirement since it does not include changes in the government's cash position.

in 1850 to 612.7 million fl. CM in 1855 at the height of the Crimean War.[1]

Over the next three years expenditure dropped to 358.5 million fl. CM, but

the Italian campaign again boosted expenditure to nearly 600 million fl.

CM in 1859. Thus, overall government expenditure varied between eight and

15 percent of GNP in the period 1855-58. War outlays and debt service

accounted for 60 to 80 percent of total government spending (Table 44).[2]

After 1856 the Monarchy's financial straits compelled it to reduce spending

outside these two areas from 167.8 to 114 million fl. CM. Approximately

55 percent of this fall arose from a cut in government investment in produc-

tive capital.

To finance the increase in overall expenditure the government relied

upon taxes, sales of crown assets, the floatation of bonds, and loans from

the National Bank. In the eleven year span 1850-1860 tax revenues increased

steadily from 161.0 to 264.6 million fl. CM (Table 43) as a result of the

introduction of new levies and rate increases in existing taxes. By 1856

taxes accounted for approximately six percent of national income. Total

---

[1]Concerning Austrian fiscal policy see Wysocki (pp. 68-104, 1973); Beer (1877, 1881); Gratz (pp. 222-309, 1949); Hübner (1849); Höfken (1862); von Czoernig (1862); von Pillersdorf (1851).

[2]Salaries, pensions and other labor costs accounted for approximately 60 percent of military outlays (Tafeln zur Statistik, 1860/65, Heft 3, Tafel 31, pp. 24-27). Purchases of commodities accounted for approximately 25 percent of the military budget. Although these may have influenced the pattern of industrialization, the overall impact upon the rate of economic growth was probably fairly low. Not so, however, for the army's purchases of labor services. Not only did military conscription capture 500,000 men (1857) or 1.5 percent of the population (3 percent of the labor force, assuming a 50 percent participation rate), but it also hindered investment in human capital by firms or by the young men themselves, since the seven year tour of military duty threatened to cut short the earnings stream such an investment would have produced. For a history of the National Bank and Austrian monetary policy during the neo-absolutist era see Pressburger (5 Vols., 1966-71); Zuckerkandl (1911); Kramar (1886); Kamitz (1949); Bachmeyer (1960); Austria k. k. Finanzministerium (1892). For economic policy in general see Matis (1973, pp. 29-44); Brusatti (1965); März and Socher (1973, pp. 324-26).

government revenues were augmented by the yield on government investments

and after 1855, the sale of government assets, such as railroads.

TABLE 9

HIGH-POWERED MONEY IN THE HABSBURG MONARCHY (EXCLUDING
LOMBARDY-VENETIA), 1849-1873
(in millions of fl. CM)

	Agio[a]	H[b]	Annual Rate of Growth (in percent)
1848	10.1		
1849	13.0	305.0	
1850	18.1	361.2	18.4
1851 (30 Nov.)	25.8	381.6	6.2
1852	19.8	349.5	-7.8
1853	10.6	321.1	-8.1
1854 (31 Oct.)	27.8	374.8	20.4
1855 (31 Oct.)	21.6	402.3	7.3
1856 (31 Oct.)	5.8	390.5	-2.9
1857 (31 Oct.)	5.5	401.2	2.7
1858 (31 Oct.)	4.1	406.2	1.0
1859 (31 Oct.)	20.6	453.9	11.7
1860 (31 Oct.)	32.2	456.0	0.5
1861 (31 Oct.)	41.8	472.4	3.6
1862	28.1	418.5	-9.9
1863	13.2	386.7	-7.6
1864	15.9	363.0	-6.1
1865	8.8	337.9	-6.9
1866	20.0	485.0	43.5
1867	24.8	522.1	7.6
1868	14.8	547.2	4.8
1869	21.3	570.3	4.2
1870	22.3	618.1	8.4
1871	20.6	658.0	6.5
1872	9.5	661.3	0.5
1873	8.1	669.5	1.2

Notes: [a]Agio denotes the average premium for silver during the calendar
year.
[b]H = sum of National Bank notes and state paper money held by
the public (including banks other than the National Bank). Values are in
millions of fl. CM and are for the end of the calendar year unless otherwise
specified.

SOURCE: Kramar (Appendix, 1886); Austria, k. k. Finanzministerium
(pp. 152-4, 1892); Bachmeyer (pp. 102-110, 1960); Austria, k. k. Statistische
Central Commission (1849-1865).

Despite the increase in revenues the government still ran substantial budget deficits in the period 1848-1866 which had to be covered by the proceeds either of bond sales or of loans from the National Bank. The proceeds of the National Bank loans usually led to an increase in the supply of high powered money. The bond issues competed in the capital market with private borrowers and may have crowded out private investment.

The adverse economic effects of the Monarchy's military policy were compounded by its exchange rate policy. Just as the Empire's military objectives dictated a rapid expansion of all forms of government debt, so too did its attempts to restore the gulden's silver parity force it, as soon as the army's needs had abated, to reduce its debt with the National Bank and to tap the capital market for additional funds. This resulted in a series of sharp and sustained declines in the rate of money growth which may have correspondingly retarded real economic activity in the Monarchy. In addition, this shift to bond finance may have augmented the crowding-out effect described above.

Thus, the Empire's monetary policy may be succintly summarized as the Sisyphean pursuit of the 1847 silver parity which the government had relinquished under the onslaught of the 1848 resolutions in favor of a flexible exchange rate. Each of its wars forced the government to abandon this aim and to tap again the National Bank for funds in order to finance its armies in the field. As soon as hostilities ceased, the National Bank began to decrease its holdings of Treasury debt and to amass silver reserves in preparation for the resumption of specie payments. The rate of money supply growth sagged sharply and in some instances became negative. The agio, the discount of the gulden from its 1847 silver parity, clearly reflected these gyrations in Habsburg monetary policy (see note 2, page 38).

Four distinct episodes can be distinguished. The first began with the revolution of 1848, the second with the Crimean War, the third with the Italian War of 1859 and the fourth with the 1866 war against Prussia and Italy.

Soon after the outbreak of the Viennese revolution in 1848, the government began to issue its own notes, abrogating the National Bank's monopoly of issue. It then suspended the convertibility of the gulden into silver. In addition, the government received short-term advances from the Bank, which in turn increased its own note issue. High powered money continued to increase until 1851, when the government began the first of its consolidation efforts in order to restore the pre-1848 parity of the gulden (see note 2, page 38). The Finance Ministry concluded an agreement with the National Bank to replace state currency with the Bank's notes (23 Feb. 1854) and to repay the state's short term debt to the Bank. To accomplish these goals it floated several bond issues, including the national loan of 1854 for 500 million gulden CM, a sum in excess of total high powered money. The fall in the money supply unleased complaints that credit was scarce, just at the time when the Grundentlastung had catapulted the agricultural sector into the money economy (Kramar, pp. 41, 51, 1886).

The outbreak of the Crimean War foiled the Austrian attempts to restore the currency's external value. The proceeds of the national loan, which took on the character of a forced levy, were absorbed by the military occupation of the Danubian principalities. The government tapped the Bank for additional loans. As a result, high powered money increased by 25 percent from the end of 1853 to 31 Oct. 1855; the agio spurted to 36 percent in May 1854 from the nine percent level of the first half of 1853.

In mid-1855 Bruck became Finance Minister with a mandate to reform the Empire's fiscal and monetary system so that the bank might resume convertibility at the pre-1848 level. Bruck planned to repay the state's debts to the bank with specie acquired by sales of state property and of bonds. In other words, the bank would replace state debt with specie reserves in its asset portfolio. Bruck attempted to limit his reform to these two items on the asset side of the bank's balance sheet; he wanted neither the bank's credit to the economy nor its note issue to decrease. Here, he was fairly successful; high powered money remained relatively constant in the years 1855-1858 and, as the ratio of specie reserves to notes in circulation increased, the exchange rate improved markedly, so that in October 1858 the National Bank was able to resume specie payments.

This also permitted Austria to join a monetary union with the Zollverein. The currency treaty of 1857 required the two areas to maintain a fixed exchange rate. Both remained on a silver standard. Such a Muenzunion had been demanded by Prussia as a precondition for Austrian entry into the Zollverein, lest a depreciating Austrian paper gulden jeopardize the tariff revenues of the entire customs federation. This agreement implied the end of Austria's monetary independence and recoupled her to the specie flow mechanism.[1] It is somewhat ironic that the treaty required a five percent devaluation of the gulden in terms of silver, after the government had undergone such strenuous efforts to regain the official silver parity.[2]

---

[1] For a discussion of monetary independence under flexible exchange rates and monetary interdependence under fixed exchange rates see Johnson (pp. 1-45, 1971).

[2] Wysocki (pp. 295-321, 1973) gives the details of the Muenzvertrag but conducts his analysis purely in political terms.

However, the Monarchy soon regained her monetary freedom, for in
April 1859 it was at war—this time against France and Piedmont over the
control of Northern Italy. The government repeated its wartime practice
of tapping the bank for advances, which the public ultimately absorbed in
the form of bank notes. Over the four months (May-August 1859) the war
lasted, the supply of high powered money jumped 27 percent before leveling
off at approximately 470 million fl. OW. The exchange rate plummeted at
the start of hostilities from an agio of nine percent to one of 41 percent
(May-June 1859) before returning to an agio of about 20 percent at year end.

The constitutional crisis of 1861 created substantial uncertainty;
a revolution in Hungary seemed imminent. This probably caused the rise in
the agio from 20 percent to nearly 50 percent (January 1861), although the
reported slump in economic activity, along with a constant supply of high
powered money, may also have contributed to this development.

Beginning in September 1861 the liberal Finance Minister, Ignaz von
Plener, mounted another drive to regulate Austria's fiscal morass and restore
the gulden's silver parity. Plener planned to increase the bank's ratio of
specie to notes in circulation both by additions to its stock of specie and
by reductions in the quantity of notes outstanding. He was eminently successful in the latter aim; the stock of high powered money fell by 29 percent in
the period September 1861 to December 1865. Although the exchange rate rose
substantially (the agio fell from 40 percent in December 1861 to two percent
in February 1866), economic activity slumped in the Monarchy. Real factors,
such as the cotton famine, the silkworm epidemic and a disastrous harvest in
1863 adversely affected income, but the contractionary monetary policy compounded
these difficulties.

TABLE 10

THE DEBT OF THE HABSBURG MONARCHY (EXCLUDING LOMBARDY-
VENETIA) HELD BY THE PUBLIC, 1848-1865
(in millions of fl. CM)

	G^P	GM^P	GNM^P	$\triangle\ GNM^P$
1848	1,126	. . .	1,126	
1849	1,256	71	1,185	59
1850	1,427	152	1,275	90
1851	1,458	194	1,264	−11
1852	1,590	156	1,434	170
1853	1,657	148	1,509	75
1854	1,897	19	1,878	369
1855	2,207	10	2,197	319
1856	2,282	8	2,274	77
1857	2,207	5	2,202	−72
1858	2,259	1	2,258	56
1859	2,418	. . .	2,418	159
1860	2,247	. . .	2,247	−171
1861	2,319	12	2,308	61
1862	2,406	13	2,393	85
1863	2,427	10	2,417	24
1864	2,477	5	2,472	55
1865	2,474	4	2,470	−2

SOURCE: Tafeln der Statistik

Notes: G^P – government debt (nominal value) held by the public excluding
Grundentlastung issues.

GM^P – state paper money held by the public.

GNM^P – government non-monetary debt held by the public. The public
excludes government offices and the National Bank. Values refer to the end
of the fiscal year (31 October until 1862, 31 December thereafter).

In 1866 war again forced the government to resort to the printing

presses of the National Bank. Within a year the supply of high powered money

rose 43 percent; the Gründerzeit boom began. Money continued to expand

rapidly until 1871; thereafter it slowed to less than a one percent annual

rate through the end of 1873. The sudden drop in the rate of monetary

expansion in 1871 suggests itself as a proximate cause of the contraction of

1873.

These gyrations in the rate of Austrian money supply growth probably obstructed the economy's upward path, or at least that of its monetary sector. Thus, the agio, or more precisely, the ambition to eliminate it, may have retarded Austrian economic growth.

So may have the substantial increase in the government's non-monetary debt. In the period 1848-1865 the amount of government bonds held by the public rose from 1.13 to 2.47 billion fl. CM, an average annual increase of 80 million fl. CM or about two percent of GNP in 1856/58 (Table 10). Approximately half the increase in the debt was concentrated in the years 1854 and 1855 when the government raised nearly 700 million fl. CM to finance its military operations in the Balkans. To the extent that these debt issues crowded out private investment, Austrian growth would have suffered.[1]

---

[1]I assume that the private sector perceived government bonds as net wealth, i.e., that it did not increase its savings to compensate for the future tax liabilities implied by the debt. Cf. Diamond (pp. 1126-50, 1965); Modigliani (pp. 730-755, 1965). The latest discussion is provided by Barro (pp. 1095-1118, 1974). Even though foreigners purchased Austrian debt (von Czoernig, p. 386, 1862), Austrian investment may have declined, if foreigners diverted resources to government bonds which they otherwise would have invested in productive capital in Austria. Williamson (pp. 636-661, 1974) presents a similar analysis of the effects of the Civil War debt on U.S. economic growth.

If one assumes that the entire increase in publicly held debt crowded out private investment, one may derive a maximum estimate of the adverse consequences of Habsburg fiscal policy. The average annual increase in the public's debt holdings was 80 million fl. CM or two percent of GNP in 1856/58. If one assumes that this represents the shortfall in private investment, crowding out would have chopped 0.7 percent per year from GNP, on the additional assumption that the capital output ratio was 3.0. After seventeen years (1848-1865), the cumulative effect of this crowding out would have lowered GNP 13 percent, approximately one-fourth the gap between German and Austro-Hungarian GNP in 1911/13. The value of 3 for the capital output ratio approximates that for England in 1832 (Deane and Cole, p. 306, 1969). This may be a bit high, given England's advanced stage of development in 1832. If so, the corresponding loss in the Monarchy's income would have been greater.

Both monetary and fiscal policy, however, took their cues from
the Monarchy's military objectives. These led the Empire into successive
conflicts which diverted resources, either through taxes or debt issues
to the public sector. As a result the Monarchy's economic growth may have
lagged. In any case, the Empire's exchange rate policy compounded the
adverse impact of its military policy.

TABLE 11

THE GERMAN MONEY SUPPLY, 1850-1873
(in millions of marks)[a]

	Banknotes	State Paper Money	Specie	Total
1850		154	1202	1356
1851	102		1207	
1852	113		1207	
1853	113		1207	
1854	119		1212	
1855	129		1260	
1856	245		1263	
1857	288		1266	
1858	320		1291	
1859	366		1364	
1860	463		1439	
1861	533		1509	
1862	521	98	1547	2166
1863	524	101	1565	2190
1864	527	104	1585	2216
1865	579	108	1602	2289
1867	637		1797	
1868	684		1821	
1869	703		1837	
1870	854		1851	
1871	1074		1885	
1872	1378	184	2189	3751
1873	1368		2472	

SOURCE: Hoffman (p. 814, 1965).

Note: [a](1 Thaler = 3 marks).

The contrast with Germany is striking, particularly for the early
1860's. The German states adhered to the silver standard throughout the period

1850-1873 and as a consequence the Germany money supply followed a smooth
upward trend, broken only in the crises of 1857 and 1866 (Table 11). In
the early 1860's Germany confronted the same obstacles in the real sector
as did the Habsburg Empire, yet its national income continued to increase
(Table 12). It is, perhaps, more than a coincidence that its money supply
also continued to expand until 1866, when the English Overend-Gurney panic
temporarily halted the growth of the money stock (Schuchardt, pp. 91-141, 1962).

TABLE 12

GERMAN NATIONAL INCOME AND GOVERNMENT DEBT, 1850-1873
(in millions of marks, 1 Thaler = 3 marks)

	National Income	Government Debt	Δ GD
1849		1393	
1850		1567	174
1851	9135	1716	149
1852	9315	1945	229
1853	9556	1981	36
1854	9801	2057	76
1855	10039	2210	153
1856	10276	2254	44
1857	10536	2268	14
1858	10811	2258	-10
1859	10961	2460	202
1860	11189	2495	35
1861	11413	2527	32
1862	11642	2543	16
1863	11796	2544	1
1864	12198	2560	16
1865	12422	2640	80
1866	12529	2833	193
1867		3035	202
1868		3359	324
1869	13572	3431	72
1870		3968	537
1871	14275	4411	443
1872	14911	3507	-904
1873	15195	3265	-242

SOURCE: Hoffmann and Müller (p. 39, 1959); Hoffmann (p. 789, 1965).

Note: All values based upon current prices.

The fiscal policies of the German states were also more conducive to economic growth. They ran much smaller budget deficits and restricted the increase in government debt to miniscule amounts. Total German government expenditures in 1850–79 never exceeded 8.2 percent of net national product even during the Franco–Prussian War of 1870 (Table 13).

TABLE 13

GERMAN GOVERNMENT EXPENDITURES AS A SHARE OF GERMAN
NET NATIONAL INCOME, 1850–1879

	Total (%)	Without Defense (%)
1850/4	6.9	5.3
1855/9	6.0	4.5
1860/4	5.8	4.5
1865/9	7.2	4.2
1870/4	8.2	4.2
1875/9	8.1	4.2

SOURCE: Hoffmann (p. 108, 1965).

Note: Net national income at current prices.

The increase in German public debt in 1849–65 was 1.25 billion marks, approximately 80 million marks per year or about half the increase in the Habsburg debt (Table 12). Of course, this placed much less of a burden on the larger German economy, particularly in the early 1850's. In 1851/56 the increase in German debt held by the public amounted to 1.2 percent of German net national income, while the increase in the public's holdings of the Habsburg Monarchy's debt totalled 4.9 percent of the Empire's 1856/58 GNP (Table 14).

TABLE 14

CHANGE IN PUBLICLY-HELD GOVERNMENT DEBT AS A PERCENTAGE
OF NATIONAL INCOME, 1851/56 to 1870/73
(in percent)

	Germany GD/NI	Habsburg Monarchy GD/NI (1856/8)
1851/56	1.2	4.9
1857/63	0.4	0.9
1864/69	1.2	
1870/73	−0.3	
1870/71	3.5	

SOURCE: Tables 10 and 11.

These differences in economic policy between Germany and the Habsburg
Empire rest, in turn, on contrasting foreign policies. The Habsburg government fought one war after another in the period 1848-66 in a vain attempt to
preserve its influence within Europe and its own territorial and political
integrity. The German states, on the other hand, successfully preserved
their neutrality through much of the period, with a consequent saving in
military expenditure.

In many ways the contrasting national compositions of the two areas
contributed to their divergent military records. Germany had a relatively
national homogeneous population; the Habsburg Empire, an assortment of ten
different nationalities. In Germany, the liberals accepted Hohenzollern
absolutism as the price of national unity and the nation acceded to Prussia's
policy of neutrality in European conflicts.

However, the Habsburgs, as the defenders of a supranational ideal in
a world of nation states, became the target of myriad national movements both

within the Monarchy and in its neighboring states. This involved the
Monarchy in a series of wars in which it repeatedly had to limp into
conflict with a fresh adversary before it could fully recover from the
last war. The government's attempt to impose an absolutist muzzle on
its nationalist movements backfired; it necessitated sharply higher police
expenditures but failed to dissolve Italian, Magyar or Czech nationalism.
Its forays into European politics in order to bolster the dynasty's control
over the Empire also failed; it lost its Italian provinces entirely, it
yielded German hegemony to Prussia, it alienated Russia and helped create
nationalist magnets for its own Serbs and Romanians in Belgrade and Bucharest.
Thus, to the extent that nationalism depressed the long lever running from
foreign policy via war and the consequent budget deficits to the crowding
out of private investment, it may be said to have obstructed the economic
growth of the Monarchy.

CHAPTER IV

CONCLUSIONS

This paper has attempted to refine the current analysis of economic
growth in the nineteenth century Habsburg Empire. It suggests that the
western half of the Empire industrialized fairly rapidly in the period 1841
to 1856/58, somewhat contrary to the assessment of the historical literature
that this had been merely a preparatory epoch for later economic growth.
The early progress seems evident from a comparison of the 1841 and 1856/58
industrial surveys, as well as from statistics concerning the output of
individual industries, the increase in the use of coal and of steam power
and the Monarchy's relatively strong trade performance, especially as an
exporter of manufactures.

The last point leads to a reconsideration of the role in the
Monarchy's economic growth of its trade reforms viz. the creation of a
unified, Monarchy-wide customs area (1850), the revisions of the external
tariff (1852, 1854) and the commercial treaty with the German Zollverein
(1853). In the opinion of many historians, these reforms laid the foundation
for the Monarchy's economic growth by exposing the backward, sheltered
Austrian economy to the rigors of foreign competition. Internally, the
establishment of a Monarchy-wide area also spurred economic growth, since
it integrated the economies of Cisleithania and Hungary.

This thesis shows that, although the two halves of the Empire had
complementary economies, the benefits of the removal of the internal customs

51

barrier were negligible since the preexisting tariff barriers were very low.
The tariff revisions of 1852 and 1854 seem to have been more a foreign
policy ploy to gain the Monarchy's entry into the Zollverein than the dawn
of a new economic era since the sharpest reductions came on goods which
Austria already exported. The silver clause of the 1854 tariff actually
pushed the whole structure back toward protectionism. The third major
trade reform, the commercial treaty with the Zollverein, also had a
negligible impact since the Habsburg Empire had a trade structure virtually
identical with that of the Zollverein. Thus, mutual tariff reductions
induced relatively small trade flows. The low levels of duty in effect
under the February Treaty on trade between the two areas also ensured that,
had the much discussed customs union between the Habsburg Empire and the
Zollverein occurred, it would have had little effect upon the economic, but
not the political, life of the two areas.

The thesis then concludes with an alternative hypothesis to help
explain the discrepancy between German and Austrian economic growth in the
nineteenth century. Rather than the failure of the Monarchy to join the
Zollverein, the Monarchy's military policy may have caused its economic
performance to lag behind that of Germany, since the wars diverted resources
away from private investment either through taxation or bond issues. The
Monarchy's attempt to restore the pre-1848 parity of the gulden as a basis
for its entry into a closer economic union with Germany compounded the
adverse impact of its military policy, since it led to sharp and sustained
declines in the rate of money growth. These probably caused temporary
reductions in the rate of real economic activity, especially in the early
1860's. In the choice of these policies nationalism--as a force which

threatened the break-up of the Monarchy both from within and from outside
its frontiers--played a predominant role. In this sense, it may have
retarded the Monarchy's economic development.

APPENDIX

TABLE 15

GROSS VALUE OF THE INDUSTRIAL PRODUCTION OF THE HABSBURG
MONARCHY (EXCLUDING LOMBARDY), 1856/58 AND 1865
(in millions of fl. OW)

| | Monarchy | | Hungarian | Cisleithania | |
	1856	1865	Share	1856	1865
Bricks, pottery, etc.	20	21	15	17	18
Glass	15	20	10	14	18
Iron, steel mfg.	70	55	20	56	44
Non-ferrous metals	30	30	30	21	21
Engineering	56	68	10	50	61
Machines	36	48			
Transport equip.	20	20			
Wood manufacturing	40	40	30	28	28
Paper and paper prods.	40	40	15	34	34
Textiles	470	445		390	413 (367)
flax and hemp	150	150	25	113	113 (67)
cotton	100	100	0	100	100
wool	130	130	10	117	117
silk	25	15	0	25	15
apparel	50	50	10	45	45
mixed fibers	15		10[a]	13	
Leather and leather prods.	100	100	30	70	70
Chemicals	25	25	25	19	19
Food, beverages, tobacco	225	250	35	146	162
Printing	70	70	10	63	63
Stonework	10		20[b]	8	
Totals	1171	1164	(20)	939	928

SOURCE: Cols. 1 and 2 Schmitt (1860; pp. 217-48, 1867) respectively.
Col. 3 Gross (1966).

Notes: [a]Hungarian share assumed to have been 10 percent.

[b]Hungarian share assumed to have been 20 percent.

TABLE 16

VALUE ADDED IN THE INDUSTRIAL PRODUCTION OF THE HABSBURG MONARCHY (EXCLUDING LOMBARDY), 1856/58
(in millions of fl. OW)

	Value added coefficient (%)		Net Output in Cisleithania[c]		Net Output in Entire Monarchy
	N. Gross	Revised[b]	N. Gross	Revised	
Bricks	60	55	10.20	9.35	11.00
Glass	75	67	10.50	9.38	10.05
Iron	45	55	25.20	30.8	38.5
Non-ferrous metals	45	39	9.45	8.19	11.70
Engineering	55	55	27.50	27.50	30.80
Manufactures of					
Wood	60	60	16.80	16.80	24.00
Paper	45	45	15.30	15.30	18.00
Textiles	46		168.82		
Linen		60		40.20 (67.80)[a]	90.00
Cotton		74		74.00	74.00
Wool		50		58.50	65.00
Silk		36		9.00	9.00
Apparel		46		20.7	23.00
Other		3		0.39	0.45
Leather	33	50	23.10	35.0	50.00
Chemicals	38	38	7.22	7.22	9.50
Food	25	25	36.50	36.50	56.25

Printing	58	58	36.54	36.54	40.60
Stonework	60	60	4.80	4.80	6.00
Totals	(44)	(51.6)	391.93	440.17 (467.77)[a]	567.85[a]

SOURCE: Gross (1966, p. 158); Schmitt (1854, 1860).

Notes: [a] inclues non-marketed linen.

[b] revisions based upon data from Schmitt (1854, 1860). For engineering, manufactures of wood, paper, chemicals, food and printing I used Gross's estimates.

[c] Cisleithania includes Venetia.

Bricks, etc., Schmitt (1854, pp. 158-9) contains the following estimates of total output and value added (Mehrwert der Arbeit) in million fl. CM, value added in parentheses: procelain 1.5 (0.75), stoneware 2.5 (0.75), tobacco pipes 0.125 (0.05), clay pots, etc. 6.0 (3.0), bricks 20.0 (12.0). Thus the gross value of output was 30.125 million fl. OW of which 16.55 million fl. CM or 55 percent comprised value added.

Glass: Schmitt (1854, pp. 162-63) puts total output at 18 million fl. CM and value added at 12 million fl. CM for a value added coefficient of 67 percent.

Iron: Schmitt (1860, pp. 151-52) contains the following estimates of total output and value added in million fl. OW in 1855, value added in parentheses: smelting and refining works (pig and wrought iron) 40 (14.4), manufactures 15 (12), small tradesmen 15 (12). Thus the gross value of output was 70 million fl. OW of which 38.4 million fl. OW or 55 percent comprised value added.

For the value added in smelting and elementary fabrication (pig and wrought iron) I have relied upon an 1858 estimate of production costs by the Association of Austrian Iron Industrialists (Denkschift der am 6 Sept. 1858 in Wien versammelten Eisen-Industriellen, Notes to Table IIb).

Non-ferrous metals: Schmitt (1854, pp. 155-56) divides this category into six sub-groups with the following values of total output and value added in millions of fl. CM (in parentheses) for 1851: gold and silver 17.15 (6.0), copper 2.5 (0.1), lead 1.0 (0.75), tin 0.427 (0.35), zinc 0.025 (0.161), alloys 2.0 (0.67). Thus the gross value of output was 23.398 million fl. CM of which 9.236 million fl. CM or 39 percent comprised value added.

Textiles (linen): Schmitt (1854, pp. 164-66) estimates the value of the industry's output at 130.75 million fl. CM, and the value of raw materials consumed at 52 million fl. CM. This implies a value added ratio of 60 percent.

Cotton: Schmitt (1854, pp. 167-8) estimates that raw materials accounted for 20.5 million fl. CM of the total output of 80 million fl. CM of the Austrian cotton industry. This yields a value added coefficient of 74 percent.

Wool: Schmitt (1854, pp. 170-71) sets the total value of industry production at 106.5 million fl. CM and the value of the raw materials consumed at 53 million fl. CM, for a value added coefficient of 50 percent.

Silk: Schmitt (1854, pp. 168-9) gives 21.75 million fl. CM as the gross value of silk textile production. Raw materials accounted for 14 million fl. CM (chiefly raw silk and wood for fuel), for a value added coefficient of 36 percent.

Clothing: value added coefficient assumed equal to Gross's coefficient for total textiles.

Other (fabrics of mixed fibers): Schmitt (1854, p. 171) puts value added at 500,000 fl. CM out of total value of 15 million fl. CM, a coefficient of three percent.

Leather: Schmitt (1854) gives the total value of production at 100 million fl. CM. Raw leather accounted for 65 million fl. of that sum. Tanning had a 50 percent value added coefficient and I have assumed a similar coefficient for the latter stages of fabrication.

Stonework: Schmitt (1854, pp. 160-61) gives a value added coefficient of 60 percent for the industry.

TABLE 17

VALUE ADDED IN THE INDUSTRIAL PRODUCTION
IN CISLEITHANIA,[a] 1841
(in millions of fl. CM)

	Net Output according to N. Gross	Revised	Gross Output according to N. Gross
Bricks	13.80	12.65	23.0
Glass	11.25	10.05	15.0
Iron	11.70	14.3	26.0
Non-ferrous metals	7.65	6.63	17.0
Engineering	3.85	3.85	7.0
Wood	0.90	0.90	1.5
Paper	2.92	2.92	5.5
Textiles	69.37		150.8
Linen		20.10 (31.92)[b]	33.5 (53.2)[b]
Cotton		29.82	40.3
Wool		31.50	63.0
Silk		5.04	14.0
Leather	12.54	19.0	38.0
Chemicals	4.18	4.18	11.0
Food, etc.	29.97	29.97	77.0
Beer and spirits	17.80	17.80	44.5
Sugar	3.08	3.08	12.3
Other	9.09	9.09	20.2
Totals	168.10	190.91 (202.73)[b]	371.8

SOURCE: Gross (1966, p. 111). Value added coefficients from Table 2 applied to Gross's figure for the gross value of production to obtain the revised net output figure.

Notes: [a]Cisleithania includes Venetia.

[b]includes the value of non-marketed linen.

59

TABLE 18

VALUE ADDED IN THE INDUSTRIAL PRODUCTION
OF CISLEITHANIA, 1841-1911/13
(in millions of fl. CM)

	1841[a]	1856/8[a]	1880	1885	1911/13
Total, current prices	200[b]	440[b]	513	623	2124
Population (millions)	19.265	20.432	21.982	22.778	28.516
Value added per capita	10.4	21.5	22.3	27.4	74.5
Price index (1913=100)	94	111[c]	81	72	91.5
Value added per capita, 1913 prices	11.0	19.4	28.8	38.0	81.4

SOURCE: For 1880, 1885 and 1911/13 see Gross (1968b, p. 67). For
1841, Table 3. Total net output excluding non-marketed linen (1.05 fl.
OW = 1 fl. CM). For 1856/58, Table 2. Total net output (revised) excluding
the value of non-marketed linen and stoneware.

Notes: [a]includes Venetia, therefore the estimates for 1856/58 and 1841
are not directly comparable with those for later years.

[b]excludes the value of non-marketed linen. Its inclusion would
boost the 1841 total to 213 million fl. OW and the 1856 total to 468 million
fl. OW. The rate of growth would remain unchanged at 3.6 percent.

[c]average of prices for industrial goods for 1856-57, Jacobs and
Richter (1935, p. 78). The use of the German price index as a deflator only
approximates the movement of Austrian prices. These deviated from German
prices due to the existence of flexible exchange rates between the two areas
after 1848 and differences in tariffs on industrial goods. Under the assumption that purchasing power parity held in 1856/58, I adjusted the Jacobs-
Richter price index for these years by the average silver premium. This would
yield a deflator of 117 and real per capita industrial value added of 18.4, for
a growth rate of 3.3 percent per annum.

The Jacobs-Richter index itself has only a restricted coverage and
may poorly reflect the movement of German industrial prices. It is limited
to intermediate products such as pig iron and yarn and also includes industrial
raw materials such as hides and coal. No attempt was made to correct for any
possible errors from this source.

TABLE 19

GROSS VALUE OF THE AGRICULTURAL PRODUCTION OF THE HABSBURG MONARCHY, 1856
(in millions of fl. CM)

	Millions of fl. CM		Millions of fl. CM
Grain		**Livestock Products**	
Wheat	219.5	Cow milk	133.5
Rye	228.4	Goat milk	8.4
Corn	128.8	Wool	60.6
Halbfrucht	75.1	Meat	
Barley	85.6	Hides and furs	
Oats	134.1		
Other grain	32.3	Total	428.6
Total	1054.2		
		Other Products	
Field Crops		Honey	9.5
		Wax	7.0
Legumes	31.3	Silk cocoons	32.5
Potatoes	97.3	Wood	89.3
Rice	5.7	Wine	141.7
Beets	10.7	Fruit	10.7
Cabbage	28.4	Chestnuts	1.0
Hay, clover	817.8	Eggs	38.1
Straw	626.0	Wild game	47.6
Tobacco	10.0		
Flax	24.3	Total	377.4
Hemp	30.9		
Flax and hemp seed	11.0		
Hops	5.7		
Total	2753.6	Grand Total: 3559.6 = 3737.5 million fl. OW	

SOURCES: <u>Tafeln zur Statistik</u> (1856); Arenstein (1862, pp. x-xiii); Schmitt (1860), pp. 118 ff.)

TABLE 20

COMMODITY OUTPUT AND GROSS NATIONAL PRODUCT OF THE
HABSBURG MONARCHY (EXCLUDING LOMBARDY), 1856/58
(in millions of fl. OW)

Value added in	Estimates		
	I	II	III
Agriculture	1991	2020	2000
Mining and smelting	184	72	70
Industry	599	570	570
Total (commodity output)	2774	2662	2640
Handicrafts, services	450		
Commerce and transportation	1080		
Gross domestic product	4324		

SOURCES: Estimate I, Schwarzer (1857, pp. 104-105). Schwarzer was
briefly Minister of Public Works in 1848 and then entered economic journalism
in the 1850's. He based his calculations upon the official statistics of
the Monarchy and his own estimates of value-added and of output of services,
commerce and transportation. Estimate II, Tables 2 and 16. Estimate III:
agriculture, average of Estimates I and II. Mining and smelting and industry,
minimum of Estimates I and II.

TABLE 21

PIG IRON PRODUCTION OF THE HABSBURG MONARCHY, 1823-1884

(in thousands of metric tons)

	Cisleithania	Hungary	Italy	Total Monarchy[a]	Total Monarchy without Italy
1823	60.227	9.985	....	....	70.212
1824	64.587	12.847	....	....	77.434
1825	58.776	12.699	....	....	71.475
1826	63.577	12.137	....	....	75.714
1827	68.655	11.974	10.009	90.638	80.629
1828	72.519	13.130	....	....	85.649
1829	74.745	15.211	4.363	94.319	89.956
1830	69.280	16.123	3.859	89.010	85.403
1831	74.978	15.039	3.989	94.006	90.017
1832	73.007	14.412	2.574	89.993	87.419
1833	74.835	19.087	5.637	99.559	93.922
1834	79.566	17.261	4.938	101.765	96.827
1835	86.194	19.708	5.742	111.644	105.902
1836	86.318	23.221	4.834	114.373	109.539
1837	95.615	19.249	3.755	118.619	114.864
1838	98.286	18.181	4.890	121.357	116.467
1839	100.576	21.987	6.672	129.235	122.563
1840	105.377	21.929	6.557	133.863	127.306
1841	110.557	23.464	8.241	142.262	134.021
1842	114.360	27.687	6.332	148.379	142.047
1843	117.857	28.065	6.444	152.366	145.922
1844	130.399	27.836	6.224	164.459	158.235
1845	133.682	31.606	6.443	171.731	165.288
1846	151.308	30.144	6.279	187.731	181.452
1847	155.451	38.344	7.513	201.308	193.795
1848	129.313	24.000	....	....	153.313
1849	125.280	24.000	....	....	149.280
1850	155.729	33.230	9.539	198.498	188.959
1851	153.748	43.378	13.246	210.372	197.126

Year					
1852	167.930	48.098	10.588	226.616	216.028
1853	180.967	56.339	9.161	246.467	237.306
1854	194.242	60.218	10.642	265.102	254.460
1855	212.569	62.708	.	.	255.277
1856	215.098	72.423	.	.	287.521
1857	231.825	80.368	5.609	317.802	312.193
1858	244.677	80.586	.	.	325.263
1859	220.128	97.214	.	317.342	.
1860	224.724	86.964	.	311.688	.
1861	230.514	84.879	.	315.393	.
1862	255.520	98.352	.	353.872	.
1863	248.414	108.202	.	356.616	.
1864	202.389	116.661	.	319.050	.
1865	190.981	101.403	.	292.384	.
1866	177.938	106.720	.	284.658	.
1867	214.878	105.555	.	320.433	.
1868	262.630	112.475	.	375.105	.
1869	278.100	127.012	.	405.112	.
1870	278.600	124.383	.	402.983	.
1871	292.736	132.902	.	425.638	.
1872	312.799	146.857	.	459.656	.
1873	371.079	163.469	.	534.548	.
1874	332.157	176.456	.	508.613	.
1875	303.449	159.704	.	463.153	.
1876	273.046	127.379	.	400.425	.
1877	259.036	128.593	.	387.629	.
1878	293.197	141.053	.	434.250	.
1879	285.839	118.321	.	404.160	.
1880	320.302	143.932	.	464.234	.
1881	379.640	164.000	.	543.640	.
1882	435.478	176.261	.	611.739	.
1883	522.400	176.456	.	698.856	.
1884	539.641	194.725	.	734.346	.

SOURCE: Kupelwieser (1886, p. 43).

Note: [a]Due to the loss of Lombardy in 1859 the figures for Columns 4 and 5 are identical for later years.

TABLE 22

DEVELOPMENT OF MECHANICAL FLAX SPINNING IN
THE HABSBURG MONARCHY, 1843-75

	Mills	Spindles	Production (mil. kg.)	Value of Production (mil. fl. OW)
1843	6	15,300	. . .	. . .
1846	. . .	. . .	39.2	37
1851	. . .	50,000	71.1	68
1854	. . .	82,000	. . .	. . .
1855	. . .	80,000	. . .	. . .
1858	. . .	120,000	84.0	75
1862	. . .	200,000	. . .	. . .
1863	. . .	210,000	. . .	. . .
1864	39	252,000	. . .	. . .
1867	. . .	300,000	. . .	. . .
1870	. . .	403,000	. . .	. . .
1875	. . .	400,000	. . .	. . .

SOURCES: 1843, von Viebahn (1846, p. 25); 1846, Hübner (1850, p. 36);
Kotelmann (1852, p. 221); 1851, Schmitt (1854, p. 165); 1854, MGS(IV, p. 96);
1855, Schmitt (1860, pp. 221-3); 1858, Schmitt (1860); 1862, Schmitt (1867,
p. 202); 1863 and 1864, Winkler (1866, p. 96); 1867, SAV (pp. 240-1); 1870,
Schmitt (1872, p. 200); 1875, Umlauft (p. 463).

TABLE 23

DEVELOPMENT OF MECHANICAL FLAX SPINNING IN MAJOR
EUROPEAN COUNTRIES, 1850-1914
(in thousands)

	1850	1863	1870	1902	1914
England and Ireland	1500	1265[b]	1600	1600	1120
France	476	563[a]	739	550	467
Austria-Hungary	50	210	400	300	390
Germany	85	136[c]	327	360	279
Belgium	120	. . .	306	250	315
Russia	50	. . .	166	240	372

SOURCES: Leiter (1916, pp. 10-11); Winkler (1866, p. 96)
Notes: [a]1861; [b]Great Britain only, 1862; [c]1862.

TABLE 24

DEVELOPMENT OF THE WOOLEN INDUSTRY IN
THE HABSBURG MONARCHY, 1845-1865

	Total Wool used (mil. kg.)	Kammgarn Factories	Spindles	Streichgarn Spindles	Production (mil. kg.)
1841	. . .	14	25,400	. . . .	. . .
1845	29.1	16	36,000	400,000	11.8
1850/2	33.6	16	39,360	. . . .	. . .
1856/58	39.2	. .	50,000	. . . .	. . .
1865	. . .		80,000	500,000	. . .

SOURCES: 1845, Hübner (1850, p. 40); von Viebahn (1846, p. 34); 1850/2, Schmitt (1854, pp. 162-4). Total yarn production for 1850/2 was 19.7 million kg. valued at 52.5 million of fl. OW. 1856/8, Schmitt (1860, pp. 223-5). In 1860 the total number of hand and mechanical spindles was 600,000. 1856/8, Amtlicher Bericht (p. 15); 1865, SAV (pp. 241-2).

TABLE 25

DEVELOPMENT OF THE SILK INDUSTRY
IN LOMBARDY, 1846-1856
(in thousand kilograms)

	1846	1856
Raw silk production	1,297	1,930
Consumption of Lombard weavers	197	207
Consumption of Lombard ribbon makers	33	67

SOURCES: 1846, Kotelmann (1852, p. 229); 1856, BNS (1856, p. 226); Frattini (1856, p. 55 ff.).

66

TABLE 26

CONSUMPTION OF RAW SILK BY VIENNESE FACTORIES, 1839-1848
(in thousands of kilograms)

Year	Value
1839	247.5
1840	298.4
1841	297.4
1842	321.7
1843	322.0
1844	323.5
1845	342.2
1846	420.6
1847	498.0
1848	202.9

SOURCE: WZ (1850, p. 2053).

TABLE 27

LEAD AND COPPER PRODUCTION OF THE HABSBURG MONARCHY, 1849-1865
(in Wiener Centner)

	Lead	Copper
1849	70,428	13,555
1850	80,263	35.745
1851	73,894	34,150
1852	75,145	45,319
1853	78,819	47,902
1854	103,347	49,862
1855	97,398	48,646
1856	88,294	45,879
1857	84,397	43,931
1858	95,744	41,227
1859	110,145	45,469
1860	125,019	47,022
1861	122,121	47,413
1862	101,650	48,071
1863	95,626	46,718
1864	101,345	50,839
1865	97,328	51,620

SOURCE: Tafeln zur Statistik (1849-1865).

TABLE 28

BEER PRODUCTION OF THE HABSBURG MONARCHY, 1841–1876
(in million hectoliters)

	Total Monarchy	Cisleithania	Hungary
1841	. . .	4.7	. . .
1844	. . .	5.0	. . .
1847	. . .	4.1	. . .
1849	. . .	5.2	. . .
1850	. . .	5.6	. . .
1851	6.1	. . .	. . .
1854	5.1	. . .	. . .
1855	5.2	. . .	. . .
1856	6.2	. . .	. . .
1857	7.2	. . .	. . .
1858	7.4	. . .	. . .
1859	7.6	. . .	. . .
1860	7.7	6.9	0.7
1861	6.8	. . .	. . .
1862	8.2	. . .	. . .
1863	8.3	. . .	. . .
1864	8.4	. . .	. . .
1865	8.4	7.8	0.6
1866	. . .	. . .	. . .
1867	7.7	7.3	0.4
1868	8.3	7.7	0.5
1869	9.0	8.4	0.6
1870	10.0	9.3	0.7
1871	10.8	10.0	0.8
1872	12.2	11.4	0.7
1873	13.4	12.7	0.8
1874	13.1	12.5	0.6
1875	12.8	12.2	0.6
1876	12.2	11.7	0.5

SOURCES: Tafeln zur Statistik (1860–1866); Statistisches Handbüchlein der österreichisch-ungarischen Monarchie (1878, p. 93).

TABLE 29

ALCOHOL PRODUCTION OF THE HABSBURG MONARCHY
(EXCLUDING DALMATIA), 1852-1859
(in millions of hectoliters)

1852	1.9
1853	2.0
1854	1.8
1855	1.9
1856	2.2
1857	2.5
1858	2.4
1859	2.6

SOURCE: Dessary (1860, p. 65).

Note: [a]50 percent alcoholic content.

TABLE 30

DEVELOPMENT OF THE SUGAR INDUSTRY IN THE HABSBURG MONARCHY, 1843-1873
(in millions of kg.)

	Production		Raw Material Use	
	Cisleithania Beets	Entire Monarchy Cane	Entire Monarchy Beets	Sugar Meal
1843	. . .	25.5	. . .	. . .
1850	16.8	. . .	. . .	. . .
1851	23.0	31.4	. . .	. . .
1852	36.0	33.6	. . .	34.9
1853	31.0	39.4[a]	. . .	37.4
1854	33.0	26.3	. . .	51.0
1855	40.0	34.7	280	29.3
1856	50.0	31.1	360	38.5
1857	58.0	22.2	440	34.6
1858	91.0	23.6	500	24.6
1859	85.0	8.1	720	26.3
1860	82.0	1.6	800	8.9
1861	80.0	1.5	780	1.8
1862	96.0	5.9	760	1.6
1863	101.0	3.3	930	6.6
1864	130.0	0.2	810	3.7
1865	128.0	. . .	1070	0.2
1866	150.0	. . .	860	. . .
1867	121.0	. . .	1140	. . .
1868	141.0	. . .	1000	. . .
1869	183.0	. . .	790	. . .
1870	221.0	. . .	1230	. . .
			1590	

TABLE 30--continued

| | Production | | Raw Material Use | |
	Cisleithania Beets	Entire Monarchy Cane	Entire Monarchy Beets	Sugar Meal
1871	213.0	. . .	1360	. . .
1872	231.0	. . .	1730	. . .
1873	242.0	. . .	1380	. . .

SOURCES: Renhardt (1974, p. 102); Rad (1862, p. 2). Yield of sugar from sugar meal assumed to have been 90 percent. Baxa (1937, pp. 136-9; 1950, pp. 54-5, 79); Kutschera (1904, p. 6); von Reden (1853, pp. 506 ff.); ZVRZV.

Note: [a]Dessary (1860).

TABLE 31

REAL EXPORTS OF MANUFACTURES FROM THE HABSBURG MONARCHY, 1851-1862
(in millions of fl. OW at 1845-47 prices)

	Cotton	Linen	Wool	Silk	Clothing	Paper and Paper Prods.	Leather Goods
1851	1.74	8.47	13.09	2.49	1.40	1.35	1.97
1852	1.99	11.26	8.42	5.56	7.27	2.17	2.67
1853	2.10	12.86	7.51	10.62	10.24	2.57	4.47
1854	2.04	6.82	9.72	6.48	8.30	2.08	3.62
1855	3.30	8.23	11.21	7.74	8.44	3.08	5.63
1856	2.67	7.86	11.75	7.87	7.82	3.96	6.48
1857	3.43	6.94	10.69	7.47	6.43	3.62	6.96
1858	4.35	6.48	7.91	5.74	5.68	3.63	6.71
1859	5.51	7.38	11.73	5.14	4.31	3.34	6.64
1860	7.95	9.56	16.09	5.18	6.40	4.39	9.58
1861	5.42	9.34	17.65	4.76	6.67	3.88	10.68
1862	3.65	8.07	17.15	4.76	7.83	4.42	7.62

	Wooden Mfgs.	Glass and Glassware	Pottery	Iron and Steel Mfgs.	Mfgs. of Non-Ferrous Metals
1851	3.10	7.61	0.26	2.36	0.91
1852	4.89	8.68	0.43	3.84	0.89
1853	6.22	9.20	0.63	4.24	0.67
1854	4.07	9.80	0.50	2.65	0.44
1855	4.49	11.37	0.67	4.61	0.75

	Transport Equipment, Land and Water	Instruments	Machinery	Notions	Chemical Products
1856	5.45	13.68	0.80	5.73	0.89
1857	5.69	15.10	0.87	6.11	1.02
1858	4.92	12.56	0.79	6.09	0.67
1859	4.31	13.54	0.78	5.87	0.64
1860	4.40	15.44	0.93	7.13	0.64
1861	4.37	12.80	0.71	13.80	0.92
1862	4.29	12.64	0.85	10.21	0.94

	Transport Equipment, Land and Water	Instruments	Machinery	Notions	Chemical Products
1851	0.71	0.26	0.10	3.75	1.00
1852	2.84	2.66	0.14	9.95	1.14
1853	4.34	3.42	0.21	14.45	1.43
1854	1.04	1.74	0.13	18.31	1.17
1855	1.64	1.43	0.20	19.59	1.39
1856	2.70	2.30	0.27	17.88	1.32
1857	2.91	2.10	0.34	17.28	1.44
1858	3.57	0.87	0.33	13.63	1.29
1859	2.93	0.76	0.53	14.75	1.56
1860	4.17	1.10	0.56	18.22	1.57
1861	4.07	1.64	1.33	26.96	1.58
1862	6.06	1.54	1.73	28.67	2.07

	Matches, etc.	Books, etc.	Flour	Brandy	Other	Total
1851	0.86	2.76	0.68	0.10	0.78	55.75
1852	0.70	2.75	0.92	0.04	1.79	81.00
1853	1.28	3.11	1.32	0.04	2.92	103.85

1854	1.50	2.10	0.85	0.28	2.17	85.81
1855	1.45	2.66	1.94	0.32	2.64	102.78
1856	1.48	2.92	2.42	1.14	2.07	109.46
1857	1.91	3.13	4.92	1.92	1.58	111.86
1858	1.70	3.24	3.64	0.72	1.61	96.13
1859	2.16	2.97	3.25	0.52	2.58	101.20
1860	2.64	2.76	4.89	1.02	3.20	127.82
1861	1.79	3.07	6.44	1.26	1.19	140.33
1862	1.91	3.34	7.09	0.57	1.19	136.60

SOURCE: Austria, Ausweise (1860, XIX part 2; 1864, XXIII, pp. XX-XXV). The years 1851 and 1852 refer to the year ending October 31 of that year. 1853 denotes the fourteen month period November 1, 1852-December 31, 1853. The years 1854 and following are calendar years.

TABLE 32

THE VALUE OF EXPORTS FROM THE HABSBURG MONARCHY IN 1863
(in thousands of fl. OW)

	Value	Share in Total (%)		Value	Share in (%)
Primary Products			**Intermediate Goods**		
Wool	46,433	15.9	Tanned Leather	1,373	0.5
Wood	28,128	9.7	Silk	9,778	3.4
Grain	12,071	4.1	Linen Yarn	4,704	1.6
Oil Seeds	2,178	0.7	Woolen Yarn	2,015	0.7
Hops	2,845	1.0	Cotton Yarn	1,020	0.4
Clover Seeds	2,307	0.8	Iron and Steel	2,943	1.0
Livestock	8,114	2.8	Non-ferrous Metals	1,227	0.4
Skins and Hides	3,903	1.3			
Feathers, etc.	2,779	1.0	Total	23,060	7.9
Gemstones	1,510	0.5			
Chemicals	1,920	0.7	**Agricultural Final**		
Flax, Hemp	2,543	0.9	**Goods**		
Coal	1,608	0.6			
Salt	878	0.3	Flour	5,709	2.0
Leaf Tobacco	1,073	0.4	Wine	1,669	0.6
Vegetables	747	0.3	Butter	905	0.3
			Other fats	235	0.1
Total	119,037	40.9	Brandy	714	0.2
			Fruit	1,508	0.5
Manufactures			Oil	167	0.1
			Cheese	376	0.1
Kurze Waren	32,801	11.3			
Woolen Goods	17,648	6.1	Total	11,283	3.9
Glass	12,129	4.2			
Linen Goods	8,942	3.1			
Leather Goods	7,910	2.7			
Iron mfgrs.	7,714	2.6			
Paper	5,381	1.8			
Clothing	6,391	2.2			
Silk Goods	5,610	1.9			

Woodware	4,341	1.5
Ships	3,140	1.1
Books	3,747	1.3
Cotton Goods	3,539	1.2
Matches, etc.	2,273	0.8
Chemical prods.	2,017	0.7
Instruments	1,625	0.6
Wagons	846	0.3
Machines	860	0.3
Wickerware	502	0.2
Total	127,416	43.8
Grand Total Listed Goods	280,796	96.4
Total Exports	291,207	100.0

SOURCE: Austria, Ausweise (1864).

TABLE 33

THE VALUE OF IMPORTS INTO THE HABSBURG MONARCHY IN 1863
(in millions of fl. OW)

	Value	Share in Total (%)		Value	Share in (%)
Primary Products			**Intermediate Goods**		
Grain	6,211	2.4	Cotton Yarn	13,908	5.5
Livestock	13,005	5.1	Linen Yarn	3,354	1.3
Dyestuffs and Tanning agents	8,614	3.4	Woolen Yarn	8,221	3.2
Wool	14,090	5.5	Silk	3,232	1.3
Cotton	33,539	13.2	Iron and Steel	2,415	1.0
Skins and Hides	9,143	3.6	Chemicals	2,720	1.1
Flax, Hemp	6,860	2.7	Corals	707	0.3
Gemstones	6,105	2.4	Non-ferrous metals	2,242	0.9
Leaf Tobacco	3,334	1.3	Raw Sugar	729	0.3
Hops	736	0.3	Leather	5,447	2.1
Oilseeds	1,444	0.6	Total	42,975	16.9
Fats	4,319	1.7			
Carving materials	2,195	0.9	**Agricultural Final Goods**		
Wood	2,809	1.1			
Coal	2,096	0.8	Coffee	15,497	6.1
Gums, Rosins	1,474	0.6	Oils	10,320	4.1
Other Seeds	1,552	0.6	Flour	2,498	1.0
Total	117,526	46.2	Tropical Fruit	2,271	0.9
			Fish	1,730	0.7
Manufactures			Spices	1,151	0.5
Books	7,638	3.0	Mfgd. Tobacco	1,223	0.5
Silk Goods	8,372	3.3	Cheese	964	0.4
Leather Goods	1,524	0.6	Wine	1,073	0.4
Iron mfgs.	4,897	1.9	Rice	380	0.1
Woolen Goods	4,420	1.7	Refined Sugar	740	0.3
Kurze-Waren	3,068	1.2	Total	38,321	15.1
Machines	2,806	1.1			

Chemical Prods.	2,721	1.1
Woodware	2,073	0.8
Paper	1,704	0.7
Cotton Goods	1,373	0.5
Total	40,596	16.0
Grand Total Listed Goods	239,418	94.2
Total Imports	254,114	100.0

SOURCE: Austria, Ausweise (1864).

TABLE 34

THE STRUCTURE OF INTRA-EMPIRE TRADE, 1846-47

	Value	Share in Total (%)
Austrian Exports to Hungary (in thousand Gulden CM)		
Refined sugar	1,829	3.1
Brandy, spirits	426	0.7
Bar iron	943	3.0
Iron and Steel mfgs.	1,772	3.0
Cotton yarn	1,609	2.7
Knitted cotton goods	658	1.1
Cotton thread	774	1.3
Woven cotton goods	18,345	30.9
Coarse linen goods	3,177	5.3
Fine woolen goods	4,971	8.4
Common woolen goods	2,628	4.4
Silk goods	2,488	4.2
Leather	1,124	1.9
Total Listed Goods	40,744	68.6
Total Trade	59,454	100.0
Hungarian Exports to Austria (in thousand fl. CM)		
Leaf Tobacco	3,025	5.4
Linseed and Rapeseed oil	371	0.7
Rapeseed	1,257	2.2
Wheat	6,731	12.0
Corn	688	1.3
Rye	827	1.5
Barley	613	1.1
Oats	1,414	2.5
Oak Apples	530	0.9
Wool	16,495	30.2
Bed feathers	374	0.7
Skins and Hides	1,502	2.7
Wine	817	1.5
Oxen and Steers	3,814	6.8
Sheep	659	1.2
Pigs	4,099	7.3
Smelted Copper	1,862	3.3
Total Listed Goods	45,528	81.3
Total Trade	56,088	100.0

SOURCE: Austria, _Ausweise_ (1853, XI, part 2).

TABLE 35

AD VALOREM TARIFF RATES ON INTRA-EMPIRE TRADE, 1850
(in percent)

	t_{HA}		$t_{A'H}$	
	(1)	(2)	(1)	(2)
Austrian Exports to Hungary				
Refined sugar	free	free	free	free
Brandy	6.9	20.8	0.9	2.5
Bar Iron	1.0	1.3	0.4	0.5
Cotton yarn (No. 30)	2.1	4.2	0.4	0.7
Cotton thread	1.6	3.9	0.3	0.6
Knitted cotton goods	0.4	---	0.2	---
Woven cotton goods	2.5	8.0	0.2	0.7
Coarse linen goods	1.3	2.3	0.2	0.2
Fine woolen goods	1.7	5.0	0.1	0.4
Common woolen goods	2.3	2.5	0.4	0.4
Silk goods	1.5	2.0	0.3	0.4
Leather	1.8	2.0	0.2	0.3
Iron and steel mfgs.	1.7	4.2	0.3	0.8
Hungarian Exports to Austria	$t_{H'A}$		t_{AH}	
Leaf tobacco	free	free	free	free
Linseed, rapeseed oil	0.4	0.5	5.0	5.9
Wheat	0.4	0.5	5.0	5.4
Corn	0.4	0.5	5.0	4.9
Rye	0.3	0.5	5.0	5.5
Barley	0.3	0.3	5.0	4.8
Oats	0.5	0.3	3.0	2.9
Oak apples	0.3	0.2	0.3	0.2
Rapeseed	0.4	---	1.2	---
Wool	free	free	0.3	0.4

TABLE 35--continued

| | $t_{H'A}$ | | t_{AH} | |
	(1)	(2)	(1)	(2)
Bed feathers	0.4	0.4	0.4	0.4
Skins and Hides	0.6	0.6	0.6	0.6
Wine	0.6	0.8	10.0	15.8
Oxen	3.8	---	5.0	---
Sheep	2.8	---	5.0	---
Pigs	3.8	---	5.0	---
Copper	free	free	free	free

SOURCES: Columns headed (1): tariff rates at official prices calculated from specific duties and official prices as given in Austria, Ausweise (1853, XI, part 2). Columns headed (2): tariff rates at current prices calculated from specific prices and wholesale prices in Pest for the following commodities: linseed and rapeseed oil, wheat, corn, rye, barley, oats, oak apples, wool, bed feathers, and wine Beiträge zur Geschichte der Preise ungarischer Landes-produkte im neunzehnten Jahrhundert (1873). Generally, the lowest quality of the product was chosen so that the tariff rate given is a maximum. For woven cotton goods: price for 7/8 Ellen wide Floridas for October 1849 (minimum price for all woven cotton goods at Reichenberg for the year October 1849-September 1850), Bericht der Handels-und Gewerbekammer Reichenberg (1852, p. 57); weight conversion of piece of 60 Ellen = 8 Zollpfund Bericht der Handels-und Gewerbekammer Prag (1854-58, p. 83). Cotton yarn price for domestic number 30 from Kramar (1886, p. 93). Prices for all other goods from Austria, k.k. Finanzministerium (1850) which relies on a survey of prices in the Monarchy from 1845-47. For an explanation of t_{HA}, $t_{A'H}$, $t_{H'A}$ and t_{AH}, see note 1, page 21.

TABLE 36

SPECIFIC TARIFF RATES OF THE HABSBURG MONARCHY, 1850–1854
(in paper fl. CM/ZZ)

	Before 1852	Feb. 1, 1852	Jan. 1, 1854	ZV
Primary Products				
Grain	——		——	——
Wheat	0.35	0.33	0.40	free
Rye	0.24	0.25	0.31	free
Corn	0.25	0.25	0.31	free
Beans	0.20	0.25	0.31	free
Peas	0.48	0.25	0.31	free
Barley	0.22	0.17	0.21	free
Oats	0.16	0.17	0.21	free
Rice				
Cleaned	1.01	0.75	0.92	npr
Uncleaned	1.01	0.25	0.31	npr
Hops	3.57	2.50	3.06	npr
Oilseeds	0.12	0.08	0.06	free
Clover seeds	0.74	0.83	0.32	free
Anis	1.03	0.75	0.92	free
Livestock				
Oxen and Steers	3.57	4.00	4.90	4.28
Cows	1.79	2.00	2.45	2.00
Young cattle	1.79	2.00	2.45	1.84
Calves	0.30	0.42	0.49	free
Sheep, Goats	0.27	0.25	0.31	free
Pigs	0.89	1.00	1.22	1.22
Piglets	0.04	0.08	0.21	free
Horses	2.68	2.00	2.45	free
Skins and Hides	0.37	0.42	free	free
Bed feathers	4.46	2.50	0.92	free
Lard	1.34	0.75	0.92	npr
Olive oil mixed w/turpentine	3.57	1.50	1.84	npr

Wood	10.%			
Firewood	0.19	0.42	0.49	free
Carpenter's	0.004	0.75	0.92	free
Charcoal, peat	0.004	free	free	free
Coal		free	free	free
Carved materials				
Whalebone	1.34	0.75	free	free
Meerschaum	4.46	0.75	free	free
Dyewoods	0.19	0.08	free	free
Gerberlohe	----	0.08	free	free
Krapp	0.38	0.10	0.12	----
Cochenille	13.84	0.75	0.92	----
Indigo	6.70	0.75	0.92	----
Gums, resins				
Terpentine	0.89	0.75	0.92	free
Gums	4.46	0.75	0.92	npr
Salt	0.46	0.42	0.49	----
Chemicals				
Potash	0.09	0.08	free	free
Sulphur	0.74	0.08	free	free
Eisenvitriol	1.03	0.42	0.49	free
Cotton	1.49	1.00	free	free
Hemp, Flax	0.22	0.08	0.04	free
Wool	0.45	0.08	free	free
Gemstones	35.71	25.00	18.36	9.18
Leaf tobacco	. . . . .under license.			u.l.
Intermediate Goods				
Chemicals				
Soda	0.19	0.42	0.40	npr
Sulphuric acid	4.46	1.50	1.50	0.92
Lead (pig)	5.63	2.50	0.49	0.46
Rolled lead	7.50	7.50	9.18	----
Pig iron	2.14	0.75	0.49	0.46
Bar iron	5.36	2.50	3.06	1.22
Rails	3.57	3.50	3.06	1.22
Steel	6.43	4.00	3.06	1.22
Sheet iron	8.57	4.00	4.90	1.84
Plows, machine parts	5.36	5.00	6.12	1.84

Zinc				
Smelted	0.37	0.42	0.49	free
Sheet	3.57	4.00	4.90	1.84
Copper				
Smelted	10.71	0.75	0.92	free
Sheet	14.29	7.50	9.18	3.06
Castings	-----	7.50	9.18	5.51
Tin, smelted	10.71	7.50	9.18	npr
Cotton yarn	8.93	8.00	7.34	3.06
Dyed	17.86	15.00	15.30	3.06
Linen yarn				
Raw machine	2.23	2.50	3.06	0.92
Bleached or dyed	4.62	12.50	15.30	9.18
Leather				
Common	7.44	7.50	9.18	3.06
Fine	22.32	15.00	15.30	3.06
Final Manufactures				
Cotton Goods				
Common	-----	55.00	48.95	npr
Middling	104.17	82.50	91.79	55.07
Fine	-----	165.00	122.38	122.38
Finest	892.86	275.00	305.95	244.76
Linen goods				
Sail material, bleached	2.23	2.50	1.84	npr
Coarse	17.86	8.25	18.36	npr
Common	37.20	22.00	48.95	npr
Middling	-----	82.50	91.79	55.07
Fine	267.86	110.00	122.38	91.79
Finest	-----	275.00	305.95	244.76
Pottery				
Coarse	0.37	0.42	0.49	free
Common	6.70	5.00	6.12	3.06
Stoneware	60.00	10.00	12.24	5.51
Porcelain, white	60.00	15.00	18.36	5.51
Fine	-----	40.00	48.95	36.71
Lead manufactures	-----	16.50	18.36	9.18

Iron Manufactures				
Coarse	10.71	5.83	6.12	3.67
Common	----	11.00	12.24	3.67
Fine	----	16.50	18.36	5.51
Manufactures of non-ferrous Metals				
Zinc and Tin	48.21	16.50	18.36	1.84
Common	----	16.50	18.36	5.51
Fine	----	16.50	18.36	5.51–18.36
Instruments	20.00	15.00	12.24	3.67
Machinery				
Wooden	10.00	15.00	18.36	npr
Cast Iron	5.00	4.00	4.90	npr
Wrought Iron	----	4.00	4.90	npr
Dry Goods and Notions				
Finest	1785.70 ¹·	660.00	305.95	npr
Fine	----	110.00	122.38	36.71–61.19
Common	----	55.00	61.19	18.36–36.71
Chemical Products				
Glue, starch	1.79–13.39	0.75	0.92	free
Dyes, etc.	93.75	15.00	18.36	free
Candles				
Wax	13.39	7.50	9.18	3.67
Stearin	25.30	4.00	6.12	3.67
Lard	5.96	2.50	3.67	3.67
Soap	3.57	2.50	3.67	npr
Matches	238.09	5.00	6.12	free
Books	4.46	3.00	3.67	free
Final Manufactures				
Woolen Goods				
Coarse	89.29	13.75	9.18	npr
Common	59.53	55.00	61.20	55.07
Middling	163.39	82.50	91.79	55.07
Printed	163.39	110.00	122.38	55.07
Fine, tull	60.00	165.00	122.38	122.38
Shawls	60.00	275.00	183.57	244.76
Finest	----	275.00	183.57	244.76

Silk Goods				
Fine	892.86	660.00	305.95	146.86
Common	321.43	275.00	183.57	91.79
Clothing				
Common	60.%	82.50	91.79	npr
Fine	60.%	165.00	183.57	npr
Finest	60.%	275.00	305.95	npr
Paper				
Coarse	0.74	0.75	0.92	free
Common	3.13	3.00	3.67	free
Fine	8.92	7.50	9.18	1.84
Finest	238.09	25.00	18.36	5.51
Wallpaper	80.36	30.00	36.71	7.04
Playing cards	————	30.00	36.71	npr
Paper goods	————	15.00	18.36	5.51
Leather Goods				
Common	44.64	25.00	18.36	9.18
Fine	44.64	50.00	48.95	18.36
Gloves	89.32	100.00	91.79	36.71
Wooden Manufactures				
Coarse	2.98	0.42	0.49	free
Common	5.21	2.50	2.45	0.92
Fine	22.32	7.50	6.12	1.84
Finest	————	15.00	18.36	5.51
Glass				
Raw	————	2.50	1.84	free
Mirror	————	2.50	1.84	0.92
Common	5.96	5.00	6.12	3.06
Middling	26.79	12.50	12.24	3.67
Fine	————	20.00	18.36	5.51
Finest	————	20.00	24.47	12.24
Coffee	11.16	10.00	12.24	npr
Sugar				
Refined	14.29	14.00	17.13	npr
Raw, for refiners	7.14	7.00	8.57	npr
Tobacco Products	. . . . . . .only under license. . . . .
Tropical Fruit				
Fine	3.57-5.36	5.00	6.12	npr
Middling	1.49-2.98	2.50	3.06	npr
Common	0.74	0.75	0.92	npr

Cheese	6.70	5.00	6.12	1.84
Fats, butter	1.34-2.23	2.50	3.06	2.66
Fish oil	0.27	0.75	0.37	npr
Olive oil	3.57	4.00	4.90	npr
Other fatty oils	2.23	1.50	1.84	0.92
Beer	0.71	0.75	0.92	npr
Spirits	4.46	7.50	9.18	npr
Flour	0.36	0.75	0.92	free

SOURCE: Calculated from Matlekovits (1877, Appendix); Kramar (1886, p. 23).

Note: npr = no preference; u.l. = under license.

TABLE 37

THE VALUE OF ZOLLVEREIN TRADE IN 1850/56
(in thousands of Taler)

	Imports	Percent	Exports	Percent
Colonial Products				
1850	34,735	16.8	3,185	0.5
1851	36,085	17.1	3,694	0.7
1852	41,302	18.4	3,710	0.2
1853	40,719	18.9	4,918	0.2
1854	44,188	16.3	5,374	0.2
1855	50,623	15.8	6,015	0.2
1856	49,505	15.4	5,349	0.2
Other Agricultural				
1850	15,407	7.5	41,663	20.0
1851	16,966	8.1	28,670	14.3
1852	30,504	13.6	27,650	12.7
1853	22,933	10.6	38,074	14.0
1854	33,581	12.2	51,475	14.3
1855	39,262	12.3	44,150	14.0
1856	43,019	13.4	43,978	13.9
Industrial Raw Materials				
1850	93,353	45.3	38,555	18.5
1851	93,245	44.3	34,919	17.4
1852	90,827	40.4	43,598	20.0
1853	91,011	42.1	45,397	16.7
1854	130,728	47.5	74,693	20.8
1855	154,570	48.3	80,834	25,6
1856	143,623	44.6	60,737	19.2
Intermediate Goods				
1850	37,119	18.0	12,850	6.2
1851	36,487	17.3	13,665	6.8
1852	35,956	16.0	15,331	7.0
1853	34,987	16.2	18,346	6.7
1854	40,017	14.5	19,009	5.3
1855	44,723	14.0	19,075	6.0
1856	51,436	16.0	22,068	7.0
Textiles				
1850	13,279	6.4	72,080	34.6
1851	14,509	6.9	76,734	38.3
1852	13,827	6.2	80,956	37.1
1853	13,635	6.3	107,310	39.5
1854	13,691	5.0	119,940	33.4
1855	15,795	4.9	104,016	32.9
1856	18,238	5.7	111,506	35.2

TABLE 37--continued

	Imports	Percent	Exports	Percent
Other Manufactures				
1850	11,809	5.7	39,539	19.0
1851	12,716	6.0	41,983	20.9
1852	11,756	5.2	45,259	20.7
1853	11,827	5.5	55,217	20.3
1854	12,669	4.6	87,502	24.4
1855	13,611	4.3	60,493	19.2
1856	14,888	4.0	72,207	22.8
Total Trade				
1850	206,213	100.0	208,483	100.0
1851	210,541	100.0	200.603	100.0
1852	224,852	100.0	218,488	100.0
1853	215,997	100.0	271,711	100.0
1854	275,701	100.0	359,380	100.0
1855	319,748	100.0	315,935	100.0
1856	321,886	100.0	317,205	100.0

SOURCE: Borries (1970, p. 60). The difference between the sum of
categories 1 through 4 and the totals in 6 represents miscellaneous items.
Percent denotes the share of the category in total imports or exports.

TABLE 38

THE VALUE OF ZOLLVEREIN IMPORTS FROM THE HABSBURG MONARCHY
ACCORDING TO ZOLLVEREIN STATISTICS, 1858
(in thousands of Taler)

Primary Products	Value	Manufactures	Value
Grain	2,715	Glass	1,308
Livestock	1,462	Linen textiles	1,678
Seeds	1,417	Woolen textiles	126
Wool	7,221	Silk Textiles	170
Feathers	1,852	Chemical products	625
Flax	436	Books	680
Skins and hides	815	Other manufactures	852
Hops	125		
Other goods	726	Total	5,439
Total	19,314		
		Agricultural Final Goods	
		Wine	271
		Butter	647
Intermediate Goods		Cheese	86
		Starch	140
Iron and Steel	290	Flour	688
Linen yarn	857	Fruit, dried	828
Woolen yarn	145	Other	286
Non-ferrous metals	84		
Tanned leather	25	Total	2,701
Silk	184		
Other goods	141		
Total	1,827		
Total Imports	29,526		

SOURCES: Quantity from Zollverein, Central Bureau (1858) and Austria, Ausweise (1858, XIX). Prices from Hubner (1861,Vol. VII, pp. 5-9).

TABLE 39

THE VALUE OF ZOLLVEREIN EXPORTS TO THE HABSBURG MONARCHY
ACCORDING TO ZOLLVEREIN STATISTICS, 1858
(in thousands of Taler)

	Value		Value
Primary Products		**Intermediate Goods**	
Grain	2,339	Cotton yarn	800
Seeds	338	Linen yarn	572
Flax	761	Woolen yarn	490
Wood	1,275	Silk	97
Skins and Hides	754	Leather	1,084
Hops	221	Copper	811
Wool	767	Zinc	78
Livestock	1,375	Tin	275
Coal	894	Lead	57
Krapp	380	Iron and steel	900
Tanning Agents	139	Other goods	207
Potash	129	Total	5,371
Other goods	438		
Total	9,811	**Agricultural Final Goods**	
		Butter	225
Manufactures		Flour	761
Paper	517	Wine, brandy, beer	135
Pottery, etc.	208	Oil	260
Silk	989	Other, foodstuffs, tobacco	349
Woolen	950	Total	1,730
Cotton	111		
Linen	70		
Woodware	647		
Books	2,076		
Instruments	181		
Glass	242		
Iron and Steel mfgs.	883		
Chemical products	589		

Kurze Waren	424
Copperware	122
Lead manufactures	12
Zincware	184
Tinware	31
Leather goods	467
Clothing	148
Other manufactures	123
Total	8,974

Total Exports 26,831

SOURCES: Same as Table 38.

TABLE 40

THE VALUE OF HABSBURG MONARCHY IMPORTS FROM THE ZOLLVEREIN
ACCORDING TO AUSTRIAN STATISTICS, 1863
(In thousands of fl. OW)

	Value	Share (%)		Value	Share (%)
Primary Products			**Intermediate Goods**		
Grain	3,114	4.6	Cotton yarn	6,327	9.3
Oil seeds	650	1.0	Linen yarn	582	0.9
Livestock	703	1.0	Woolen yarn	2,491	3.7
Other seeds	1,058	1.6	Iron and Steel	1,136	1.7
Skins and Hides	1,638	2.4	Lead	122	0.2
Wax	181	0.3	Tin	306	0.4
Bristles	169	0.2	Copper, brass	1,083	1.6
Flax, Hemp	2,799	4.1	Zinc	431	0.6
Wool, raw	938	1.4	Other	52	0.1
Wood	2,350	3.5	Leather	2,041	3.0
Krapp	228	0.3	Chemicals	571	0.8
Garacine	620	0.9	Other goods	2	---
Dyewood extract	521	0.8	Total	15,144	22.3
Coal	1,544	2.3			
Hops	630	0.9	**Agricultural Final Goods**		
Remnants	97	0.1	Wine	104	0.2
Stones	79	0.1	Bread, etc.	217	0.2
Other products	1,494	2.2	Oils	2,474	3.6
Total	18,815	27.7	Fruit and vegetables	548	0.8
			Flour	2,442	3.6
Manufactures			Butter	104	0.1
Cotton	357	0.5	Mfg. tobacco	427	0.6
Linen	88	0.1	Sugar, refined	81	0.1
Wool	1,872	2.8	Spirits	357	0.5
Silk	2,632	3.9	Mineral Water	99	0.1
Clothing	719	1.1	Other goods	186	0.3
Wax cloth	72	0.1	Total	7,038	10.3

Paper	1,028	1.5
Leather goods	1,055	1.6
Woodware	1,514	2.2
Glass	341	0.5
Whalebone prods.	120	0.2
Pottery, etc.	528	0.8
Iron and Steel mfgs.	3,497	5.1
Machines	2,508	3.7
Kurze Waren	1,405	2.1
Instruments	457	0.7
Chemical prods.	2,033	3.0
Books	6,171	9.1
Non-ferrous metal	208	0.3
Other manufactures	359	0.5
Total	26,965	39.7
Total Imports	67,961	100.0

SOURCES: Quantity from Zollverein, Central Bureau (1863) and Austria, Ausweise (1864, XXIV). Prices from Austria, Ausweise (1864, XXIV).

TABLE 41

THE VALUE OF HABSBURG MONARCHY EXPORTS TO THE ZOLLVEREIN ACCORDING TO AUSTRIAN STATISTICS, 1863
(in thousands of fl. OW)

	Value	Share (%)		Value	Share (%)
Primary Products			**Intermediate Goods**		
Wool, raw	23,977	25.5	Cotton yarn	377	0.4
Wood	15,536	16.5	Linen yarn	4,472	4.7
Grain	7,758	8.2	Woolen yarn	1,863	2.0
Oil seeds	2,069	2.2	Silk	545	0.6
Clover seeds	1,980	2.1	Iron and Steel	329	0.4
Hops	1,346	1.4	Non-ferrous metals	403	0.4
Livestock	4,351	4.6	Leather	121	0.1
Feathers	2,359	2.5	Terpentine	214	0.2
Skins and Hides	2,311	2.5	Other goods	309	0.3
Coal	219	0.2			
Graphite	885	0.9	Total	8,632	9.2
Flax, Hemp	1,587	1.7			
Remnants	225	0.2	**Agricultural Final Goods**		
Potash	256	0.3			
Weinstein, roh	237	0.2	Butter	515	0.5
Other products	1,008	1.1	Wine	237	0.3
			Cheese	198	0.2
Total	66,103	70.2	Flour, etc.	1,549	1.6
			Fruit and vegetables	1,334	1.4
Manufactures			Mineral water	238	0.3
			Other goods	265	0.3
Books	1,935	2.1			
Matches, etc.	730	0.8	Total	4,336	4.6
Linen goods	1,753	1.9			
Glass	2,046	2.2			
Woodware	1,525	1.6			
Leather goods	295	0.3			
Paper	809	0.9			
Woolen goods	367	0.4			

Silk goods	265	0.3
Pottery, etc.	123	0.1
Iron and Steel mfgs.	2,771	2.9
Kurze Waren	881	0.9
Other manufactures	1,582	1.7
Total	15,083	16.0
Total Exports	94,154	100.0

SOURCE: Quantity from Zollverein, Central Bureau (1863) and Austria, Austria, _Ausweise_ (1864, XXIV). Prices from Austria, _Ausweise_ (1864, XXIV).

TABLE 42

AD VALOREM TARIFF RATES OF THE ZOLLVEREIN ON IMPORTS FROM THE HABSBURG MONARCHY AND FROM THE REST OF THE WORLD, 1858
(in percent)

Primary Products

	General Tariff	Austria (February Treaty)
Wheat	2.9	—
Rye	3.3	—
Barley	1.3	—
Oats	1.7	—
Anis	8.0	—
Hemp	1.0	—
Flax	1.0	—
Poppy	0.8	—
Rapeseed	0.8	—
Clover	0.8	—
Other	1.7	—
Horses	1.5	2.7
Oxen	10.0	3.3
Cows	10.0	5.6
Young cattle	16.7	—
Calves	1.9	4.9
Pigs, fattened	7.1	—
Pigs, lean	16.7	—
Piglets	33.3	—
Sheep	11.1	—
Wool	—	—
Firewood	4.2	—
Other	0.9-3.5	8.3
Hops	8.3	0.4
Bed feathers	0.4	—
Flax, Hemp	0.9	—
Skins and Hides	—	—

Intermediate Goods

	General Tariff	Austria (February Treaty)
Pig iron	30.3	12.5
Wrought iron	42.9	17.9
Rails	54.5	24.4
Steel	15.5	6.1
Wire	50.0	13.4
Sections	42.9	14.3
Sheet	40.0	17.5
Linen yarn, machine	4.0	—
Linen yarn, hand	0.4	—
Woolen yarn	0.6	0.6
Cotton yarn	9.4	5.5
Silk yarn	0.1	—
Twisted silk yarn	1.1	1.1
Copper	1.6	—
Zinc	14.3	—
Tin	—	—
Lead	3.1	3.1
Common leather	12.5	4.4
Fine leather	6.7	1.5

Final Manufactures		
Textiles		
Cotton	33.3	20.0
Fine silk	8.5	6.2
Common silk	13.8	12.5
Printed wool	33.3	20.0
Unprinted wool	15.0	15.0
Linen, unbleached	4.4	--
Linen, bleached	13.3	13.3
Ribbons	10.0	10.0
Lace	6.0	3.0
Paper, unsized	10.0	--
Paper, sized	25.0	5.0
Gold and silver paper	10.0	3.2
Wallpaper	20.0	4.0
Paper goods	10.0	3.2
Common leather goods	14.3	7.1
Fine leather goods	11.0	5.5
Gloves	29.3	14.0
Staves, cooperage	8.3	--
Ordinary mfgs. of wood	15.0	5.0
Fine mfgs. of wood	20.0	6.3
Furniture, cushioned	10.0	10.0
Coarse machines	5.0	--
Glass, coarse	3.3	--
White, unpatterned glass	10.0	5.8
Window and plate glass	10.0	5.8
White, moulded glass	20.0	6.7
Mirror glass	26.7	10.0
Unpolished glass	1.6	--
Colored glass	27.7	9.3
Coarse pottery	8.3	--
Stoneware	25.0	8.8
Stoneware, colored	20.0	6.3
Porcelain, white	16.7	5.3
Porcelain, colored	12.5	2.5
Lead mfgs., common	16.7	16.7
Lead mfgs., fine	40.0	20.0
Cast iron, coarse	12.5	6.3
Cast iron, common	75.0	25.0
Cast iron, fine	40.0	12.7

Agricultural Final Goods	60.0	60.0
Wine	60.0	60.0
Butter	12.6	5.4
Cheese	18.3	5.0
Flour	6.3	--
Fruit	6.3	--

Manufactures of		
Non-ferrous Metals	62.5	19.8
Zinc	14.3	14.3
Tin	12.5	4.2
Copper	6.0	2.0
Instruments		
Dry Goods and Notions	40.0	17.5
Gold and silver	21.0	10.5
Mother of pearl, etc.	11.1	--
Chemical products	0.5	--
Books		

SOURCES: Tariff rates from Zollverein, Central Bureau (1858). Prices from Hubner (1861, VII, pp. 5-9).

TABLE 43

GOVERNMENT REVENUES OF THE HABSBURG MONARCHY, 1850-1860
(in millions of fl. CM)

| | Taxes | | Income | | | Other | | Total |
	Indirect	Direct	Industrial Enterprises	Fund	Sales of Assets	Revenues	Total	Taxes
1850	95.6	65.4	5.1	10.6	0.1	19.4	196.2	161.0
1851	109.2	70.5	5.4	11.3	0.1	22.0	218.5	179.7
1852	122.4	79.5	4.8	12.0	0.2	13.4	232.3	201.9
1853	130.3	84.7	2.2	11.3	0.5	8.1	237.1	215.0
1854	133.3	85.6	7.1	10.6	0.1	8.8	245.5	218.9
1855	139.2	88.0	9.4	10.3	27.9	11.6	286.4	227.2
1856	148.9	92.1	9.4	10.1	23.7	7.9	292.1	241.0
1857	152.4	94.8	7.1	9.9	31.0	28.8	324.0	247.2
1858	158.8	94.5	4.5	10.0	19.4	10.9	398.1	253.3
1859	148.6	94.4	7.3	9.2	90.9	31.5	381.9	243.0
1860	169.6	95.0	8.4	---	77.5	31.4	381.9	264.6

SOURCE: Hübner (1861, VII, p. 101).

TABLE 44

GOVERNMENT EXPENDITURES OF THE HABSBURG MONARCHY, 1850-1860

(in millions of fl. CM)

| | Debt Service | War | Ministries | | | | Productive Capital | Total | Total excluding War and Debt Service |
			Interior (police)	Justice	Finance	Other			
1850	120.2	126.2	20.4	11.0	16.6	23.6	17.3	343.4	97.0
1851	123.8	122.5	26.5	17.5	20.9	25.2	19.1	369.5	123.2
1852	154.1	115.9	26.8	18.5	25.2	27.4	18.6	395.7	125.7
1853	93.1	119.3	30.9	18.1	26.3	28.8	21.4	348.3	135.9
1854	86.8	208.7	39.6	17.3	25.1	29.4	27.1	438.1	142.6
1855	245.6	216.0	31.8	15.4	25.8	32.4	34.3	612.7	151.1
1856	132.2	123.8	39.2	15.4	28.2	36.7	36.7	423.8	167.8
1857	145.0	123.0	40.0	15.9	27.1	38.8	30.7	427.7	159.7
1858	114.3	105.8	37.6	15.6	27.1	33.3	20.2	358.5	138.4
1859	177.7	286.9	47.7	14.6	24.8	17.2	18.9	595.9	131.3
1860	205.1	128.2	43.1	13.6	23.0	15.7	6.3	447.3	114.0

SOURCE: Hübner (1861, VII, p. 102). Other Ministries include Education, Commerce and Foreign as well as the expenditures of the Court and the Cabinet.

LEGEND

CISLEITHANIA

1. Tirol and Voralberg
2. Salzburg
3. Carinthia
4. Carniola
5. Coastlands
6. Styria
7. Upper Austria
8. Lower Austria
9. Bohemia
10. Moravia
11. Silesia
12. Krakau (annexed to Galicia in 1846, formerly a republic)
13. Galicia
14. Bukowina (part of Galicia until 1849)

LANDS OF THE HUNGARIAN CROWN

21. Hungary
22. Croatia-Slavonia
23. Transylvania

ITALIAN PROVINCES

31. Lombardy
32. Venetia

OTHER ADMINISTRATIVE DIVISION

41. Dalmatia

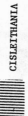

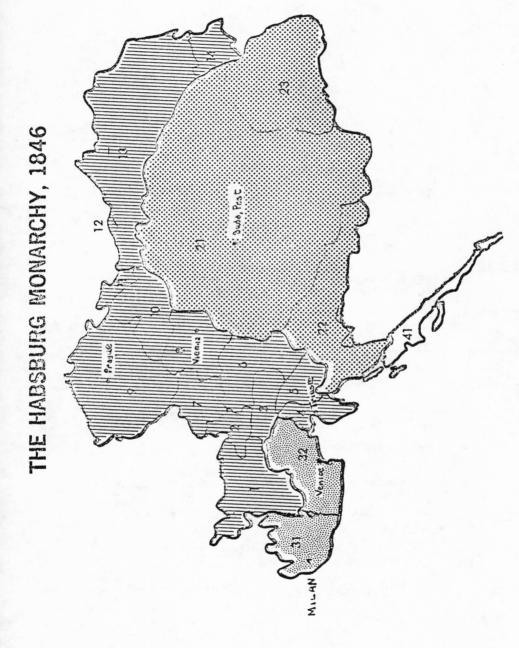

THE HABSBURG MONARCHY, 1846

BIBLIOGRAPHY

Adelmann, G. "Strukturwandlungen der rheinischen Leinen-und Baumwollgewerbe
     zu Beginn der Industrialisierung." Vierteljahresschrift für Sozial-und
     Wirtschaftsgeschichte 53 (1966): 162-84.

Andics, E. Metternich und die Frage Ungarns. Budapest: Akademiai Kiado, 1973.

Arenstein, J. Austria at the International Exhibition of 1862. Vienna:
     Hof-und Staatsdruckerei, 1862.

Äusserung der Repräsentanten der kärntnerischen Bleiproduktion über die vom
     hohen Handelsministerium aufgestellte Frage, bezüglich auf den
     Anschluss an den deutschen Zollverein. Villach: F. F. Hoffman, 1848.

Äusserung der Repräsentanten der kärnt. Eisenindustrie über die vom hohen
     Handels-Ministerium angestellte Frage über den Anschluss an den
     deutschen Zollverein. Klagenfurt: Kleinmayr, 1848.

Austria, k. k. Finanzministerium. Ausweise über den auswärtigen
     Handel Österreichs. Vienna: Hof-und Staatsdruckerei, 1841-1865.

_____. Denkschrift über das Papiergeldwesen der österreichisch-ungarischen
     Monarchie. Vienna: Hof-und Staatsdruckerei, 1892.

_____. Statistische Tabellen zur Währungsfrage. Vienna: Hof-und
     Staatsdruckerei, 1892.

_____. Tafeln zur Statistik des Steuerwesens im österreichischen
     Kaiserstaate. Vienna: Hof-und Staatsdruckerei, 1858.

Austria, k. k. Handelsministerium. Der neue allgemeine österreischische
     Zolltarif. Vienna: Hof-und·Staatsdruckerei, 1851.

Austria, k. k. Statistische Central-Commission. Mittheilungen aus dem
     Gebiete der Statistik. Vienna: 1852-1874.

_____. Statistisch-administrative Vorträge. Vienna: Hof-und Staats-
     druckerei, 1867.

_____. Statistisches Handbüchlein der österreichischen Monarchie.
     Vienna: Hof-und Staatsdruckerei, 1861.

_____. Statistisches Handbüchlein der österreichisch-ungarischen
     Monarchie. Vienna: Hof-und Staatsdruckerei, 1878.

102

Austria, k. k. Statistische Central-Commission. Tafeln zur Statistik der österreichischen Monarchie. Vienna: Hof-und Staatsdruckerei, 1841-1865.

Bachmeyer, O. Die Geschichte der österreichischen Währungspolitik. Vienna: Manz, 1960.

Barany, G. Stephen Széchenyi and the Awakening of Hungarian Nationalism, 1791-1841. Princeton: Princeton University Press, 1968.

Barro, R. J. "Are Government Bonds Net Wealth?" Journal of Political Economy 82 (1974): 1095-1118.

Batra, R. N. Studies in the Pure Theory of International Trade. London: Macmillan, 1973.

Bauer, O. Die Nationalitätenfrage und die Sozialdemokratie, 2nd ed. Vienna: Verlag der Wiener Volksbuchhandlung, 1924.

Baxa, J. Die Zuckererzeugung 1600-1850. Vienna: Leipnik Lundenberger Zuckerfabrik, 1937.

_____. Studien zur Geschichte der Zuckerindustrie in den Ländern des ehemaligen Österreich. Vienna: Universum, 1950.

Baxa, J. and Bruhns, G. Zucker im Leben der Völker. Berlin: Bartens, 1967.

Beck, L. Die Geschichte des Eisens, 5 Vols. Braunschweig: Vieweg, 1884-1903.

Beer, A. Die österreichische Handelspolitik im neunzehnten Jahrhundert. Vienna: Manz, 1891.

_____. Der Staatshaushalt Österreich-Ungarns seit 1868. Prague: Tempsky, 1881.

Beiträge zur Geschichte der Preise ungarischer Landesprodukte im neunzehnten Jahrhundert. Budapest: Handelskammer, 1873.

Benedikt, H. "Der deutsche Zollverein und Österreich." Der Donauraum 6 (1961): 25-34, 93-94.

Berend, I. T. and Ranki, G. Hungary: A Century of Economic Development. Newton Abbot: David and Charles, 1974.

_____. "Nationaleinkommen und Kapitalakkumulation in Ungarn 1867-1914." Studia Historia 52 (1970): 11-34.

Bericht der Handels-und Gewerbekammer in . . . an das hohe k.k. Ministerium für Handel, Gewerbe und öffentliche Bauten über den Zustand der Industrie, des Handels und der Verkehrsmittel im Jahre . . .
Agram, 1852, 1853, 1854-56, 1857-59.
Brünn, 1852, 1863, 1864, 1865.

Bericht der Handels-und Gewerbekammer in . . . an das hohe k. k. Ministerium
  für Handel, Gewerbe und öffentliche Bauten über den Zustand der
  Industrie, des Handels und der Verkehrsmittel im Jahre . . .
  Budapest, 1852-53, 1854, 1855-56, 1857-59, 1870-75.
  Budweis, 1851, 1853, 1854-56, 1857-59, 1870-75.
  Czernowitz, 1851, 1861, 1862-71.
  Eger, 1852, 1858, 1863.
  Graz, 1852, 1853, 1854-56.
  Olmütz, 1851, 1857-59.
  Prag, 1851, 1852, 1854-58.
  Reichenberg, 1852, 1856, 1857-60, 1861-63, 1864-66.
  Wien, 1850, 1851, 1852, 1853, 1854-56, 1857-60, 1861-66.

Bienengräber, A. Statistik des Verkehrs und Verbrauchs im Zollverein für
  die Jahre 1842-1864. Berlin: Duncher, 1868.

Böhme, H. Deutschlands Weg zur Grossmacht: Studien zum Verhältnis von
  Wirtschaft und Staat während der Reichsgründungszeit 1848-1881.
  Cologne, 1966.

_____. Probleme der Reichsgründungszeit 1848-1879. Cologne: Kiepenheuer
  and Witsch, 1968.

_____. Prolegomena zu einer Sozial- und Wirtschaftsgeschichte Deutsch-
  lands im 19. und 20. Jahrhundert. Frankfurt a.M.: Suhrkamp, 1972.

Bollettino di notizie statistische italiane e straniere e delle più importanti
  invenzione e scoperte o progresso dell'industria e delle utili
  cognizioni. Milan: 1850-58.

Bondi, G. "Zur Geschichte der 'kleindeutschen' Lösung 1866-1871." Jahrbuch
  für Wirtschaftsgeschichte II (1966): 11-33.

Borchardt, K. "Grundriss der deutschen Wirtschaftsgeschichte." Kompendium
  der Volkswirtschaftslehre, Vol. 1. Göttingen: Vandenhoeck &
  Ruprecht, 1967, pp. 346-95.

Bormann, F. A. Die Ursachen des Verfalls der Leinen-und Baumwollindustrie
  in den deutschen Zollvereins-Staaten und Vorschläge zu ihrer Hebung.
  Berlin: Grieben, 1852.

Borries, B. v. Deutschlands Aussenhandel 1836 bis 1856. Stuttgart: G.
  Fischer, 1970.

Brusatti, A. "Österreich am Vorabend des industriellen Zeitalters." Wirtschaftsgeschichte Österreichs. Vienna: Hirt, 1971, pp. 135-50.

_____. Wirtschaftspolitik vom Josephinismus zum Ständesstaat. Vienna:
  Jupiter, 1965.

_____. (ed.) Die wirtschaftliche Entwicklung. Vienna: Akademie der
  Wissenschaften, 1973. (Die Habsburgermonarchie, Vol. 1.)

Charmatz, R. Geschichte der auswärtigen Politik Österreichs im 19. Jahrhundert. 2 Vols. Leipzig: Teubner, 1914.

_____. Minister Freiherr von Bruck, Der Vorkämpfer Mitteleuropas. Leipzig: Hirzel, 1916.

Czörnig, K. Fhr. v. Österreichs Neugestaltung 1848-1857. Vienna: Hof-und Staatsdruckerei, 1858.

_____. Das österreichische Budget für 1862. Vienna: Hof-und Staatsdruckerei, 1862.

Deane, P. and Cole, W. A. British Economic Growth, 1688-1959. 2nd. ed. Cambridge: Cambridge University Press, 1969.

Denkschrift der am 6. September 1858 in Wien versammelten Eisenindustriellen. Vienna: Wallishausser, 1858.

Denkschrift des böhmischen Gewerbevereins über den Anschluss Österreichs an den teutschen Zollverein. Prague: Thabor, 1848.

Denkschrift zur Erläuterung des Entwurfs eines zu vereinbarenden gemeinschaftlichen Zolltarifs zwischen Österreich und dem deutschen Zollverein. Vienna: Hof-und Staatsdruckerei, 1863.

Dessary, A. "Bier-Studien aus Österreich, eine finanziell-volkswirtschaftliche Abhandlung." Österreichische Vierteljahresschrift für Rechts- und Staatswissenschaft 8 (1861): 191-228.

_____. "Die Branntweinindustrie und die Branntweinsteuer in Österreich." Österreichische Vierteljahresschrift für Rechts- und Staatswissenschaft 6 (1860): 55-102.

_____. "Ergebnisse einer Enquête über die dermaligen Zustände der Rübenzuckerfabrikation in Österreich." Österreichische Vierteljahresschrift für Rechts- und Staatswissenschaft 6 (1860): 187-218.

Diamond, P. A. "National Debt in a Neo-Classical Growth Model." American Economic Review 55 (1965): 1126-50.

Eddie, S. M. "The Terms of Trade as a Tax on Agriculture: Hungary's Trade with Austria, 1883-1913." Journal of Economic History 32 (1972): 298-315.

Entwurf eines im Sinne der österreichischen Vorschläge vom 10. Juli 1862 zwischen Österreich und dem deutschen Zollvereine zu vereinbarenden gemeinschaftlichen Zolltarifs. Vienna: Hof-und Staatsdruckerei, 1863.

Fellner, F. v. Das Volkseinkommen Österreichs und Ungarns. Vienna: Manz, 1917.

Fenyes, A. Ungarn in Vormärz. Leipzig: Herbig, 1851.

Frattini, G. Storia e statistica della industria manufatturiera in
   Lombardia. Milan: Bernardoni, 1856.

Der Freihafen Triest und die österreichische Industrie. Vienna: Tendler,
   1850.

Friese, F. M. Übersicht der Roheisenproduktion. Vienna: Waldheim, 1870.

Glaser, J. C. Die Handelspolitik Deutschlands und Österreichs nach ihren
   Grundlagen und in ihrem Verhältnis zu einander. Berlin: Heymann, 1850.

Good, D. F. "Stagnation and Take-Off in Austria, 1873-1913." Economic
   History Review N.S. 27, (1974): 72-87.

_____. "Financial Institutions and Economic Growth: The Evidence from
   Pre-1914 Austria." Ph.D. dissertation, University of Pennsylvania
   1972.

Gratz, A. "Die österreichische Finanzpolitik von 1848 bis 1948." Mayer
   (1949): 222-309.

Gross, N. T. "Industrialization in Austria in the Nineteenth Century." Ph.D.
   dissertation, University of California, Berkeley, 1966.

_____. "An Estimate of Industrial Product in Austria in 1841." Journal
   of Economic History 28 (1968a):80-101.

_____. "Austrian Industrial Statistics, 1880/85 and 1911/13." Zeitschrift
   für die gesamte Staatswissenschaft 224 (1968b): 35-69.

_____. "The Industrial Revolution in the Habsburg Monarchy, 1750-1914."
   C. M. Cipolla, ed., Fontana Economic History of Europe, Vol. 4, Ch. 5,
   (1973).

_____. "Economic Growth and the Consumption of Coal in Austria and
   Hungary, 1831-1913." Journal of Economic History 31 (1971): 898-916.

Grubel, H. G. and Lloyd, P. J. Intra-Industry Trade: The Theory and Measure-
   ment of International Trade in Differentiated Products. New York:
   Wiley, 1975.

Grunzel, J. "Die Baumwollindustrie." Die Grossindustrie Österreichs. Vienna:
   Hof-und Staatsdruckerei 4 (1898): 193-204.

_____. Handelspolitik und Ausgleich in Österreich-Ungarn. Vienna:
   Manz, 1912.

Hain, J. Handbuch der Statistik des österreichischen Kaiserstaates, 2 Vols.
   Vienna: Tendler, 1853.

Hanak, P. "Die bürgerliche Umgestaltung der Monarchie und der Ausgleich
   von 1867." Studia Historia 52 (1970): 191-231.

Hanak, P. "Hungary in the Austro-Hungarian Monarchy: Preponderance of Dependency?" Austrian History Yearbook 3 (1967) part 1: 260-302.

Handels-Archiv. Sammlung der neuen auf Handel-und Schiffahrt bezüglichen Gesetze und Verordnungen . . . und statistische Materialien. Delbruck, R. and Hegel, J. (eds.): Berlin, 1847-55.

Hardach, K. "Some Remarks on German Economic Historiography and its Understanding of the Industrial Revolution in Germany." Journal of Economic History 1 (1972): 37-99.

Harpke, A. Die Seiden-Industrie der Gegenwart. Vienna: n. ö. Gewerbeverein, 1876.

Henking, H. "Vortrag." Zeitschrift des niederösterreichischen Gewerbevereins 13 July, 1850.

Hertz, F. The Economic Problem of the Danubian States. A Study on Economic Nationalism. London, 1947.

Heym, G. "Die österreichische Schafwollwaren-Industrie." Österreichische Revue 2, Bd. 1 (1864): 157-79.

Hock, C. Fhr. v. "Die Verhandlungen über ein österreichisch-deutsches Zollbundnis 1849 bis 1864." Österreichische Revue 2, Bd. 1 (1864): 43-64; Bd. 2: 49-73; Bd. 3: 39-73.

_____. Gegen den ungarischen Schutzverein und seine Tendenzen. Leipzig: Barth, 1845.

Hoffmann, W. G., (ed.) Untersuchungen zum Wachstum der deutschen Wirtschaft. Tübingen: Mohr, 1971.

_____. Das Wachstum der deutschen Wirtschaft seit der Mitte des 19ten Jahrhunderts. Berlin: Springer, 1965.

Hoffmann, W. G. and Müller, J. H. Das deutsche Volkseinkommen 1851-1957. Tübingen: Mohr, 1959.

Höfken, G. Deutschlands Zoll-und Handelseinigung mit Hinblick auf die österreichische Zollreform und die Dresdener Conferenzen. Regensburg: Manz, 1851.

_____. Die österreichischen Finanzprobleme bezüglich Bank, Valuta und Deficit. Leipzig: Brockhaus, 1862.

Hübner, O. Österreichs Finanzlage und seine Hilfsquellen. Vienna: Jasper, Hügel and Manz, 1849.

_____. Die Zoll-Einigung und die Industrie des Zollvereins und Österreichs. Berlin: Decker, 1850.

Hübner, O. (ed.) Jahrbuch für Volkswirthschaft und Statistik. Berlin: 1852–1863.

Industrie und Zolltarif in Österreich. Vienna: Manz, 1859.

Jacobs, A. and Richter, H. Die Grosshandelspreise in Deutschland von 1792 bis 1934. Berlin, 1935. (Vierteljahreshefte zur Konjunkturforschung, Sonderheft 37.)

Johnson, H. G. "A Monetary Approach to the Balance of Payments Theory." Journal of Financial and Quantitative Analysis 8 (1971): 1–45.

_____. "Optimal Trade Intervention in the Presence of Domestic Distoritions." R. E. Caves; Kenen, P. B.; and Johnson, H. G., (eds.) Trade, Growth and the Balance of Payments. Amsterdam: North-Holland, 1965, pp. 3–34.

Jones, R. W. "Tariffs, Trade and General Equilibrium: Comment." American Economic Review 59 (1969): 418–26.

_____. "The Theory of Effective Protection and Substitution." Journal of International Economics 1 (1971).

Kamitz, R. "Die österreichische Geld-und Währungspolitik 1848–1948." Mayer, 1949, pp. 127–221.

Kann, R. A. The Multinational Empire: Nationalism and National Reform in the Habsburg Monarchy 1848–1918. 2 Vols. New York: Columbia University Press, 1950.

_____. The Habsburg Empire: A Study in Integration and Disintegration. New York: Praeger, 1957.

Katus, L. "Economic Growth in Hungary during the Age of Dualism (1867–1913)." Studia Historia 52 (1970): 35–127.

Kautz, J. Entwickelungsgeschichte der volkswirtschaftlichen Ideen in Ungarn und deren Einfluss auf das Gemeinwesen. Budapest: Grill, 1876.

Knoth, H. "Seide und Seidenwarenerzeugung in Österreich." Ph.D. dissertation, Hochschule für Welthandel, Vienna, 1947.

Kossuth, L. Ungarns Anschluss an den deutschen Zollverband. Leipzig: W. Einhorn, 1842.

Kotelmann, A. Vergleichende statistische Übersicht über die landwirthschaft-lichen und industriellen Verhältnisse Oestreichs und der deutschen Staaten. Berlin: Enslin, 1852.

Kramar, K. Das Papiergeld Österreichs seit 1848. Leipzig: Duncker & Humblot, 1886.

Kubenik, J. U. C. Die Einwirkung der gegenwärtigen Zollsätze auf die Baumwollindustrie in Österreich. Vienna: Gerold, 1863.

Kupelwieser, F. "Die Entwicklung der Eisenproduction in den letzten Decennien." Zeitschrift des österreichischen Ingenieur-und Architekten-Vereines 38 (1886): 36-50.

Kutschera, E. Der Centralverein für die Rübenzuckerindustrie in der österr.-ungar. Monarchie 1854-1904. Festschrift. Vienna: Sieger, 1904.

Lang, L. Hundert Jahre Zollpolitik. Vienna: k.u.k. Hof-Buchdruckerei, 1906.

Leiter, H. Die Leinen-, Hanf- und Jute-Industrie Österreich-Ungarns. Vienna: Hölzel, 1916.

Mamroth, K. Die Entwicklung der österreichisch-deutschen Handelsbeziehungen vom Entstehen der Zollvereinsbestrebungen bis zum Ende der ausschliesslichen Zollbegünstigungen (1849-1865). Berlin, 1887.

März, E. Österreichische Industrie-und Bankpolitik in der Zeit Franz Josephs I. Vienna: Europa, 1968.

_____. "Wirtschafts-und Finanzprobleme im alten Österreich." Wirtschaftspolitische Blätter 1 (December, 1954): 32-34.

_____. "Besonderheiten in der Entwicklung des österreichischen Bankwesens." Schmollers Jahrbuch 77 (1957): 189-206.

_____. "Die historischen Voraussetzungen des Credit-Mobilier Bankwesens." Schmollers Jahrbuch 79 (1959): 573-89.

März, E. and Socher, K. "Währung und Banken in Cisleithanien." Brusatti (1973): 323-68.

Matis, H. "Nationalitätenfrage und Wirtschaft in der Habsburgermonarchie." Der Donauraum 15 (1970): 171-202.

_____. Österreichs Wirtschaft 1848-1913. Berlin: Duncker & Humblot, 1972.

_____. "Die Wirtschaft der Franzisko-Josephischen Epoche." Wirtschaftsgeschichte Österreichs. Vienna: Hirt, 1971, pp. 151-184.

_____. "Leitlinien der österreichischen Wirtschaftspolitik." Brusatti (1973): 29-44.

Matlekovits, A. Die Zollpolitik der österreichisch-ungarischen Monarchie von 1850 bis zur Gegenwart. Budapest: Franklin, 1877.

Mayer, H. (ed.) Hundert Jahre österreichischer Wirtschaftsentwicklung 1848-1948. Vienna: Springer, 1949.

Migerka, V. Rückblicke auf die Schafwollwarenindustrie Brünns von 1765-1864. Brünn: Winiker, 1866.

Mitchell, B. R. "Statistical Appendix." C. M. Cipolla (ed.) Fontana Economic History of Europe, Vol. 5.

Modigliani, F. "Long Run Implications of Alternative Fiscal Policies and the Burden of the National Debt." Economic Journal 71 (1965): 730-755.

Mudge, E. R. and Hayes, J. L. "Reports on Wool and Manufactures of Wool." Reports of the United States Commissioners to the Paris Universal Exhibition 1867. Washington, D.C.: Government Printing Office, 1868.

Mühleder, F. "Die Schottenfelder Seidenindustrie 1820-1850." PH.D. dissertation, Phil. Fak. University of Vienna, 1952.

Mussa, M. "Tariffs and the Distribution of Income: The Importance of Factor Specificity, Substitutability, and Intensity in the Short and Long Run." Journal of Political Economy 82 (1974): 1191-1203.

Neumann-Spallart, F. X. v. Österreich und der Zollverein in den letzten funfundzwanzig Jahren. Vienna: Gerold, (1864a).

_____. Österreichs Handelspolitik in der Vergangenheit, Gegenwart und Zukunft. Vienna: Gerold, (1864b).

Novotny, J. "Zur Problematik des Beginns der industriellen Revolution in der Slovakei." Historia 4 (1962): 129-89.

Oechelhäuser, W. Der Fortbestand des Zollvereins und die Handelseinigung mit Österreich. Frankfurt a.M.: Bronner, 1851.

_____. Vergleichende Statistik der Eisenindustrie aller Länder. Berlin: Veit, 1852.

Offergeld, W. Die Grundlagen und Ursachen der industriellen Entwicklung Ungarns. Jena: G. Fischer, 1914.

Pacher von Theinburg, G. Entwicklung, volkswirtschaftliche Werth- und Lebensbedingungen der Baumwollspinnerei in Österreich-Ungarn. Vienna: k.k. Handelsministerium, 1891.

Pillersdorff, F. X. v. Die österreichischen Finanzen, 3rd ed. Vienna: Jasper, Hügel & Manz, 1851.

Pressburger, S. Das österreichische Noteninstitut 1816-1966. 6 Vols. Vienna: österreichische Nationalbank, 1966-71.

Pulsky, F. (ed.) Aktenstücke zur Geschichte des ungarischen Schutzvereins. Leipzig: Brockhaus, 1847.

111

Purs, J. "Die Entwicklung des Kapitalismus in der Landwirtschaft der böhmischen Länder in der Zeit 1849 bis 1879." Jahrbuch für Wirtschaftsgeschichte III (1963): 31-96.

_____. "The Industrial Revolution in the Czech Lands." Historia 2 (1960): 183-272.

_____. "The Situation of the Working Class in the Czech Lands in the Phase of the Expansion and the Completion of the Industrial Revolution." Historia 6 (1963): 145-237.

Rad, J. C. Colonial-oder Rübenzucker, welcher von beiden verdient in Österreich einen grösseren Schutz? Vienna: Gerold, 1862.

_____. Beleuchtung der Zuckerfrage im neuen Zolltarifs-Entwurf vom österreichischen Standpunkte. Vienna: Sieger, 1864.

_____. Adressenbuch der Rübenzuckerfabriken und Colonial-Zuckerraffinerien aller Länder Europas. Vienna: Sieger, 1868.

Rapporto della camera di commercio e d'industria della provincia di Bergamo sullo stato dell'industria e del commercio della propria provincia negli anni . . . 1852; 1854-1855-1856.

Rapporto della camera di commercio e d'industria della provincia di Como all'Eccelsio Imperiale Regio Ministero del Commercio, dell'Industria e delle Pubbliche Costruzione sullo stato dell'industria e del commercio della propria provincia negli anni, 1854-1855-1856.

Rapporto della camera di commercio e d'industria della provincia di Milano all'Eccelsio I.R. Ministero del Commercio, dell'Industria e delle Publiche Costruzione sullo stato dell'industria e del commercio della propria provincia negli anni 1852-53.

Rapporto generale intorno alla produzione ed al commercio della provincia veronese negli anni 1854-1855-1856 innalzato all'Eccelsio Imperiale Regio Ministero del Commercio in Vienna dalla Camera di Commercio e d'Industria in Verona.

Reden, F. W. v. Denkschrift über die österreichische Gewerbe-Austellung in Wien 1845. Berlin: Schröder, 1846.

_____. Deutschland und das übrige Europa. Wiesbaden: Kriedel & Niedner, 1854.

Redlich, J. Das österreichische Staats-und Reichsproblem. 2 Vols. Leipzig, 1920-26.

Relazione storica agricola-commerciale industriale della provincia di Cremona pel triennio 1854-1855-1856 all'Eccelsio I.R. Ministero del Commercio, delle Industrie e delle Publiche Costruzione dalle Camera di Commercio e delle Industrie di Cremona.

Renhardt, M. "Die Entwicklung der österreichisch-ungarischen Rübenzucker-industrie von ihren Anfangen bis 1914." Ph.D. dissertation, Phil. Fak., University of Vienna, 1975.

Rosthorn, J. Treatise on the Iron Trade of Carinthia. Vienna: Überreuter, 1865.

Rudolph, R. L. "Austrian Industrialization: A Case Study in Leisurely Economic Growth." Sozialismus, Geschichte und Wirtschaft. Festschrift für Eduard Marz. Vienna: Europa, 1973, pp. 249-63.

Schieder, T. "Von Deutschen Bund zum Deutschen Reich." Gebhardts Handbuch der deutschen Geschichte III, pp. 95-192.

Schmitt, F. Statistik des österreichischen Kaiserstaates, 1st. ed. Vienna: Tendler, 1854.

_____. Statistik des österreichischen Kaiserstaates. 2nd ed. Vienna: Tendler, 1860.

_____. Statistik des österreichischen Kaiserstaates. 3rd ed. Vienna: Gerold, 1867.

_____. Statistik des österreichischen Kaiserstaates. 4th ed. Vienna: Gerold, 1872.

Schuchardt, J. "Die Wirtschaftskrise vom Jahre 1866 in Deutschland." Jahrbuch für Wirtschaftsgeschichte II (1962): 91-141.

Schwarzer, E. v. Geld und Gut in Neu-Österreich. Vienna: Wallishausser, 1857.

Sieghart, R. Zolltrennung und Zolleinheit: Die Geschichte der österreichisch-ungarischen Zwischenzollinie. Vienna: Manz, 1915.

Silbermann, H. Die Seide. 2 Vols. Dresden: Kühtmann, 1897.

Tambor, J. Seidenbau und Seidenindustrie in Italien. Berlin: Springer, 1929.

Die Tarifreform in Österreich. Vienna: Gerold, 1859.

Der österreichische und Zollvereinstarif. Eine vergleichende Zusammenstellung. Vienna: Hof-und Staatsdruckerei, 1856.

Taylor, A. J. P. The Struggle for Mastery in Europe, 1848-1919. London: Oxford University Press, 1973.

Tilly, R. "The Political Economy of Public Finance and the Industrialization of Prussia." Journal of Economic History 26 (1966): 484-97.

Tremel, F. Wirtschafts-und Sozialgeschichte Österreichs. Vienna: Deuticke, 1969.

Treue, W. Gesellschaft, Wirtschaft und Technik Deutschlands im 19. Jahrhundert. Munich: dtv, 1975.

Umlauft, F. Die österreichisch-ungarische Monarchie. Geographisch-statistisches Handbuch. 3rd ed. Vienna: 1897.

Umrisse einer möglichen Reform in Ungarn. Leipzig: 1833.

Viebahn, G. W. v. Über Leinen und Wollmanufakturen, deren Ursprung, Umfang und Leistungen in Deutschland, deren Werth und Fortschritte. Berlin: Reimarus, 1846.

Verhandlungen der Versammlung zur Berathung des Zolltarifs-Entwurfes. Vienna: Hof-und Staatsdruckerei, 1852.

Winkler, A. Der Flachsbau und die Leinenindustrie in Irland im Vergleich mit Preussen und dem Zollverein. Berlin: Schweigger, 1866.

Winter, J. "Über den Schmuggel im österreichischen Kaiserstaate." Zeitschrift des niederösterreichischen Gewerbevereins 18 (May 1850).

Wolf, F. "Die Tulpenbewegung in Ungarn." Ph.D. dissertation, Phil. Fak., University of Vienna, 1973.

Worliczek, E. "Aussenhandel des österreichischen Zollgebietes 1839-1850." 2 Vols. Ph.D. dissertation, Phil. Fak., University of Vienna, 1970.

Wysocki, J. "Machtgegensätze in einer Währungsunion." Kredit und Kapital 6 (1973): 295-321.

Yeager, L. V. "Fluctuating Exchange Rates in the Nineteenth Century: The Experience of Austria and Russia." R. A. Mundell and Swoboda, A.K., (eds.) Monetary Problems in the International Economy. Chicago: University of Chicago Press, 1969, pp. 61-89.

Zeitschrift des niederösterreichischen Gewerbevereins. Vienna: 1849-51.

Zeitschrift des Vereins für die Rübenzuckerindustrie im Zollverein. Berlin: 1850-1863.

Die Zoll-und Handelseinigung zwischen Deutschland und Österreich. Leipzig: Jackowitz, 1850.

Zollenquête in Österreich. Vienna: Wallishausser, 1859.

Zöllner, E. Geschichte Österreichs. Vienna: Verlag für Geschichte und Politik, 1970.

Zollverein. Central Bureau. Statistische Übersichten über Waaren-Verkehr und Zoll-Ertrag im deutschen Zollverein. Berlin: 1850-64.

Zorn, W. "Die wirtschaftliche Integration Kleindeutschlands in den
        1860er Jahren und die Reichsgründung." <u>Historische Zeitschrift</u>
        206 (1973): 304-34.

_____. "Wirtschafts-und sozialgeschichtliche Zusammenhänge der
        deutschen Reichsgründungszeit 1850-1879." <u>Historische Zeitschrift</u>
        197 (1963): 318-42.

Zuckerkandl, W. "The Austro-Hungarian Bank." U.S. Monetary Commission.
        <u>Banking in Russia, Austria-Hungary, the Netherlands and Japan</u>.
        Washington, D. C.: Government Printing Office, 1911, pp. 55-118.

DISSERTATIONS IN EUROPEAN ECONOMIC HISTORY

An Arno Press Collection

Atkin, John Michael. **British Overseas Investment, 1918-1931** (Doctoral Dissertation, University of London, 1968). 1977

Brosselin, Arlette. **Les Forêts De La Côte D'Or Au XIXème Siècle, et L'Utilisation De Leurs Produits** (Doctoral Thesis, Université de Dijon, 1973). 1977

Brumont, Francis. **La Bureba A L'Époque De Philippe II** (Doctoral Dissertation, Université de Toulouse, 1974). 1977

Cohen, Jon S. **Finance and Industrialization in Italy, 1894-1914** (Doctoral Dissertation, University of California, Berkeley, 1966). 1977

Dagneau, Jacques. **Les Agences Régionales Du Crédit Lyonnais, Années 1870-1914** (Doctoral Thesis, Université de Paris-VIII, 1975). 1977

Dennis, Kenneth G. **'Competition' in the History of Economic Thought** (Doctoral Dissertation, Oxford University, 1975). 1977

Desert, Gabriel. **Une Société Rurale Au XIXe Siècle:** Les Paysans Du Calvados, 1815-1895 (Doctoral Dissertation, Université de Paris, Sorbonne, 1971). 1977

Fierain, Jacques. **Les Raffineries De Sucre Des Ports En France:** XIXe -- début du XXe siècles (Doctoral Dissertation, Université de Nantes, 1974). 1977

Goreux, Louis-Marie. **Agricultural Productivity and Economic Development in France, 1852-1950** (Doctoral Dissertation, University of Chicago, 1955). With the Revised French Version. 1977

Guignet, Philippe. **Mines, Manufactures et Ouvriers Du Valenciennois Au XVIIIe Siècle** (Doctoral Dissertation, Université de Lille III, 1976). Two vols. in one. 1977

Haines, Michael R. **Economic-Demographic Interrelations in Developing Agricultural Regions:** A Case Study of Prussian Upper Silesia, 1840-1914 (Doctoral Dissertation, University of Pennsylvania, 1971). 1977

Hohorst, Gerd. **Wirtschaftswachstum Und Bevölkerungsentwicklung In Preussen 1816 Bis 1914** (Doctoral Dissertation, University of Münster, 1977). 1977

Huertas, Thomas Francis. **Economic Growth and Economic Policy in a Multinational Setting:** The Habsburg Monarchy, 1841-1865 (Doctoral Dissertation, University of Chicago, 1977). 1977

Jankowski, Manfred. **Public Policy in Industrial Growth:** The Case of the Early Ruhr Mining Region, 1766-1865 (Doctoral Dissertation, University of Wisconsin, 1969). 1977

Jefferys, James B. **Business Organisation in Great Britain, 1856-1914** (Doctoral Dissertation, University of London, 1938). 1977

Kirchhain, Günter. **Das Wachstum Der Deutschen Baumwollindustrie Im 19. Jahrhundert** (Doctoral Dissertation, University of Münster, 1973). 1977

Von Laer, Hermann. **Industrialisierung Und Qualität Der Arbeit Eine Bildungsökonomische Untersuchung Für Das 19. Jahrhundert** (Doctoral Dissertation, University of Münster, 1975). 1977

Lee, W. R. **Population Growth, Economic Development and Social Change in Bavaria, 1750-1850** (Revised Doctoral Dissertation, University of Oxford, 1972). 1977

LeVeen, E. Phillip. **British Slave Trade Suppression Policies, 1821-1865** (Doctoral Dissertation, University of Chicago, 1972). 1977

Metzer, Jacob. **Some Economic Aspects of Railroad Development in Tsarist Russia** (Doctoral Dissertation, University of Chicago, 1972). 1977

Moe, Thorvald. **Demographic Developments and Economic Growth in Norway, 1740-1940** (Doctoral Dissertation, Stanford University, 1970). 1977

Mueller, Reinhold C. **The Procuratori di San Marco and the Venetian Credit Market:** A Study of the Development of Credit and Banking in the Trecento (Doctoral Dissertation, Johns Hopkins University, 1969). 1977

Neuburger, Hugh. **German Banks and German Economic Growth from Unification to World War I** (Doctoral Dissertation, University of Chicago, 1974). 1977

Newell, William Henry. **Population Change and Agricultural Developments in Nineteenth Century France** (Doctoral Dissertation, University of Pennsylvania, 1971). 1977

Saly, Pierre. **La Politique Des Grands Travaux En France, 1929-1939** (Doctoral Dissertation, Université de Paris VIII, Vincennes, 1975). 1977

Shrimpton, Colin. **The Landed Society and the Farming Community of Essex in the Late Eighteenth and Early Nineteenth Centuries** (Doctoral Dissertation, Cambridge University, 1965). 1977

Tortella[-Casares], Gabriel. **Banking, Railroads, and Industry in Spain, 1829-1874** (Doctoral Dissertation, University of Wisconsin, 1972). 1977

Viallon, Jean-Baptiste. **La Croissance Agricole En France Et En Bourgogne De 1850 A Nos Jours** (Doctoral Dissertation, Université de Dijon, 1976). 1977

Villiers, Patrick. **Le Commerce Colonial Atlantique Et La Guerre D'Indépendance Des États Unis D'Amérique, 1778-1783** (Doctoral Dissertation, Université de Paris I, Pantheon-Sorbonne, 1975). 1977

Walters, R. H. **The Economic and Business History of the South Wales Steam Coal Industry, 1840-1914** (Doctoral Dissertation, Oxford University, 1975). 1977

DATE DUE

N ~~OCT 02 1988~~	
N ~~DEC 9 1988~~	
~~NOV 2 1992~~	
~~JUN 1 0 1999~~	

MP 728